4

DIAGRAM

4

DIAGRAM

**EDITED BY
ANDER
MONSON**

NEW MICHIGAN PRESS

TUCSON

ARIZONA

—

DIAGRAM

is not and never has been
a solo enterprise.

—

Our editors have included:

Sarah Blackman, Megan Campbell, T Fleischmann, Steve Franklin, Heidi Gotz, Dolly Laninga, Ander Monson, Pablo Peschiera, Heather Price-Wright, Emma Ramey, Christopher Roman, Mike Salisbury, Michael Sheehan, Katie Jean Shinkle, Lauren Slaughter, and Nicole Walker.

The journal would not be possible without their brains and bodies. So: thanks to them.

—

Find us online at:

THEDIAGRAM.COM

DIAGRAM 4

Ander Monson, Editor.

 First Edition. Cover & interior design by Ander Monson.

Published in 2012 by NEW MICHIGAN PRESS.
Paper ISBN: 978-1-934832-33-2.

Much of the material contained herein originally appeared in *DIAGRAM*, a magazine of text, art, and schematic, which can be found online at <thediagram.com>.

Source materials for images are noted in the index page at the end of the book. We have tried, to the best of our ability, to locate and procure permission for the images used herein. If you are the copyright holder for any image, please contact us at nmp@thediagram.com and we will update the permission in our next printing.

Particular thanks to Heather Price-Wright for her help in assembling this anthology.

The cover image is from Howard C. Warren and Leonard Carmichael, *Elements of Human Psychology*, Houghton Mifflin, 1930.

thediagram.com
newmichiganpress.com

EDITOR@THEDIAGRAM.COM • NMP@THEDIAGRAM.COM

CONTENTS | CONTRIBUTORS

CONTENTS | CONTRIBUTORS | CONTINUED

CONTENTS | CONTRIBUTORS | CONTINUED

AN INEXPENSIVE, NOISELESS MEMORY APPARATUS

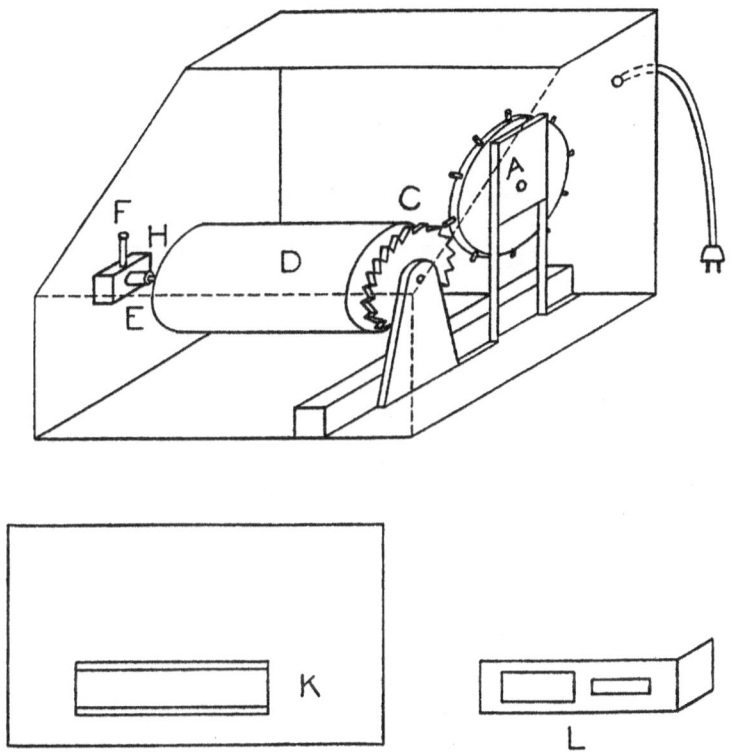

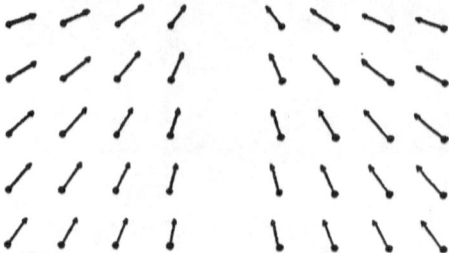

FIG. 110. SOCIAL POLARITY IN AN AUDI-
ENCE — CONDITION A

The attentive responses are all directed toward
the speaker S. Facilitating stimuli from the re-
sponses peripherally observed by each individual
in his companions assist in maintaining this com-
plete polarity.

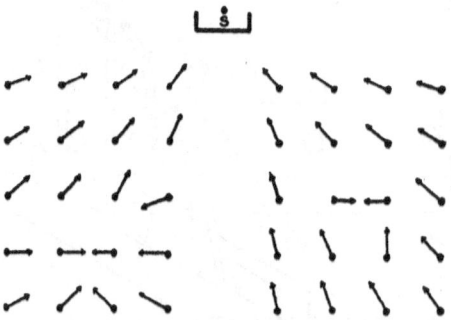

FIG. 111. SOCIAL POLARITY IN AN AUDI-
ENCE — CONDITION B

An audience in which lesser polarizing centers
have developed.

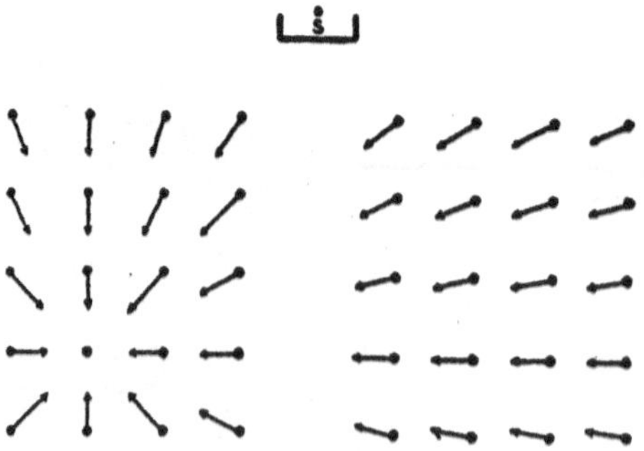

FIG. 112. SOCIAL POLARITY IN AN AUDI-
ENCE — CONDITION C

The polarity in an audience which has been
completely diverted from the speaker S to an in-
dividual C in the audience who has now become
the center of polarity.

Marcia Aldrich / *The Making of Mothers: Portraits*

THE LAUGH OF MEDUSA

This one's a mother who with each passing year becomes more selfless. This is a mother who is dropping everything of hers to do her daughter's bidding. At her daughter's bidding, this is a mother who is passing away into selflessness, more and more, more and more she is dropping everything that is hers, to buy groceries, to take her daughter clothes shopping, to keep her cupboards appealing.

This is a mother who more and more is asking if her daughter needs anything. Care and worry, care and worry, the giver, the care giver, the wart, the worry wart. Always giving, never taking. To her daughter this is a mother who is becoming old, tired, and weary. This is one who is napping in the back seat of cars, dozing in movies. This is a mother who can't stay awake.

But sometimes when she is not making her cupboards appealing, when she isn't dropping everything that is hers, she begins laughing and the laugh that is coming out of her gets louder and louder and she can't stop the laugh and the laugh becomes all there is coming out of her, and the daughter struggles to understand her mother's laugh, she struggles to understand what is coming out of her selfless mother, the one who is always asking her what she needs. She wants the mother to control herself because the laughing is getting louder and louder until the mother is disappearing inside the laugh and the daughter wants the laugh to stop.

THE WHITE GODDESS

This is a mother who thinks she should be found in the kitchen morning, noon, and night. This is one who thinks she should be an appliance, a permanent fixture like a microwave, ready to spring into use when one of her hungry daughters wanders into the kitchen. She thinks she shouldn't look like an appliance, all hard and cold and made of steel, but she should

be *like* an appliance with buttons that her daughters can push. On/
off. On/off. This is a mother who thinks she should be standing in the
kitchen, ready and waiting, in a white apron. This is a mother who thinks
she should wear pearls when she is cooking. A theme of white. This is a
mother who thinks these white things but gets the family's dinner from a
drive thru. This is a mother who can't stand in the kitchen because she is
standing in a bank counting other people's money. This is a mother who
fingers the dollar bills of strangers and thinks about where she is supposed
to be so that her daughters could find her morning, noon, and night, but
she never is. This is a mother who thinks about snow.

THE ELEMENTARY STRUCTURES OF KINSHIP

The rhythm of the mother's chopping onions hurts her daughter's soul.
    Chop. Chop. Chop. Pause.
    Hurt.
    The top of this mother's lip curls before the difficulty of the onion
    What is the difficulty of this onion, the daughter thinks, and why are
her eyes tearing up. Is it from the milky sap of the onion or the skin of the
mother? Chop. Chop. Chop. Pause.
    Hurt.
    The mother looks up from her onion to her daughter and wipes her
eyes. She, too, has tears. The daughter thinks—are my mother's tears
caused by the onion or has she read my mind? Does my mother know that
she irritates my soul?
    The mother holds out the knife to her daughter: "Will you chop
awhile? My eyes," she says.
    The daughter takes the knife silently from her mother and begins chop-
ping. Chop. Chop. Chop. Pause.
    Hurt.

This is a mother who can't finish her sentences and wishes she could but she is perpetually stranded in the middle of a blue veined thought, one flash propels her forward into the morning to the cries echoing from inside the open bedroom door and another flash turns her back in a circle to midnight and the porch where her own mother once called her to come home, no stroke sees her safely to shore to the end of the white corridor of time, no stroke straightens out the serpentine course of rescues and mistakes, the family all tucked tightly into their respective beds, no matter how hard this mother presses her temples her thoughts loop from cry to call a catalogue of loss, from bed to bed, moment to moment in a score of moments as the wind is always moving, touching but never resting, each air draft inseparable pushing along in an upward current into a sky that loves her.

LOVE SONG: THE REPRODUCTION OF MOTHERING (1)

This is a mother who still holds her daughter's hand when they're walking down the street. Her daughter is 18 years old. This is a mother who wants her daughter to look and act and be just like her. This is a daughter who does not resist what her mother wants. As the years pass this is a daughter who is becoming her mother. This is a mother who is always receding into the background. This is a mother who is always refilling platters, empty-ing trash, washing dishes. This is a daughter who with each passing year is receding into the background, watching her brother from the wings doing his tricks, clapping along with her mother and others. This is a mother who wears little Sunday school white gloves to bed to keep her hands in-nocent. This is a daughter who in time will too.

This is a mother who, as she is walking home from work after a long day, eats the sorrow that is seeping out of the windows of parked cars, leaking out of the averted eyes of the passerby, oozing from the cracks of the sidewalk. This is a mother who is getting fat with the world's sorrow. This is a mother to whom stories snake out of the dense ivy that would make you weep if you could hear them. This is a mother who doesn't turn away from what makes her weep—the story of the child who sat on her front stoop waiting for her parents to come home until the cement froze over with ice; the story of the child who disappeared with the bottle of milk her mother sent her to fetch; the story of the mother who lost her daughter when the ice broke on the river her daughter was skating. This is a mother who is a poet, though no one knows it, not even the mother.

LOVE SONG: THE REPRODUCTION OF MOTHERING (2)

This is a mother who when she was a girl was afraid of the mother. The mother turned down the sheets of her bed through soft ferns of moonlight while the father turned the pages of newspaper under bright lamp light. As a girl she heard the mother breathing through the open window and she was afraid. The mother brushed the girl's hair and polished her shoes. She learned how to cook the meals the girl liked. Yet each night when the mother filled the tub with hot clean water and called the girl to come home with *It's time and the water is running*, the girl stepped back through the trees.

Now the girl has become a mother herself. There is no part of her now that is not a mother. There was a person before she became a mother. She writes about that person, visits photographs in which she is depicted. She sees the fear in her face like a trapped animal. But now as a mother she steps out of the trees and feels exposed. She calls her daughter to come home, *it's time and the water is running*, and she is afraid her daughter won't come.

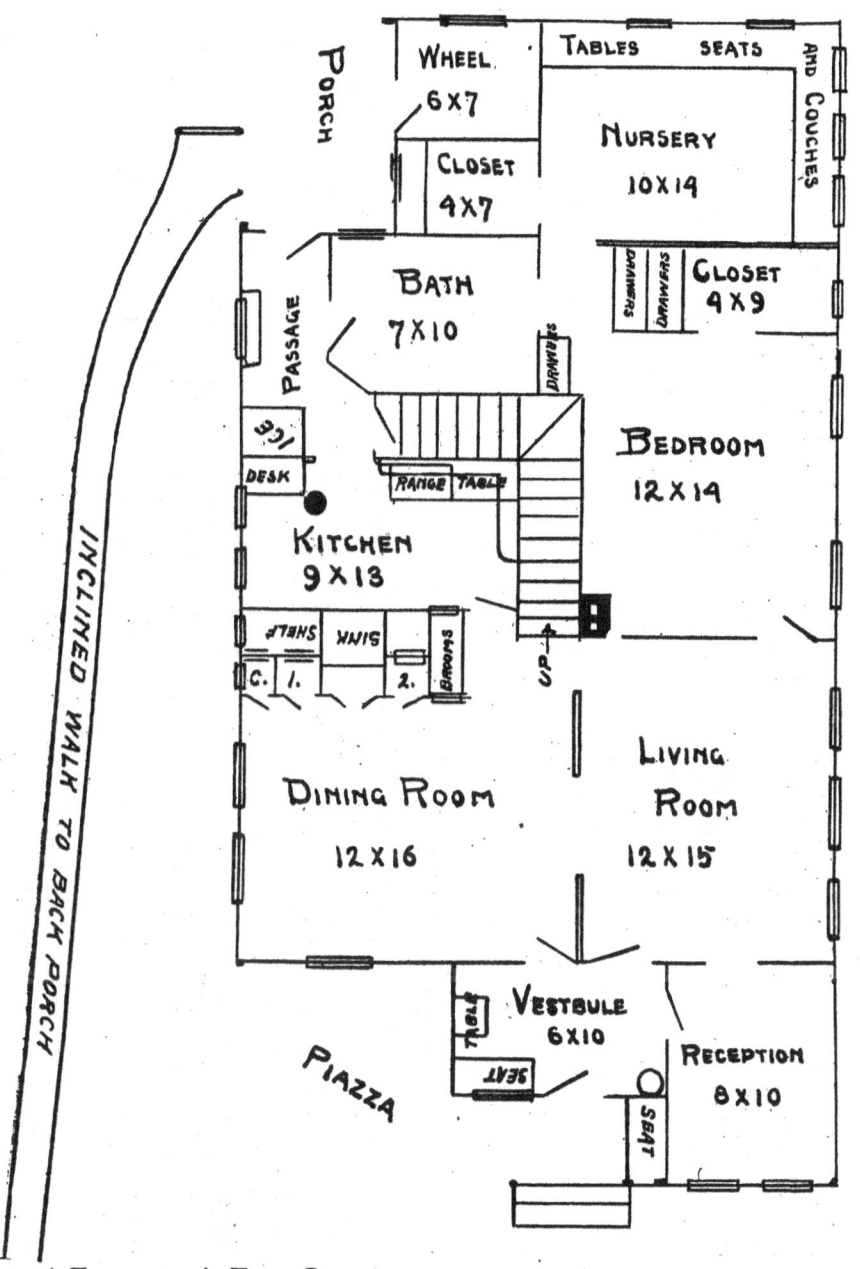

A HOUSEKEEPER'S HOUSE PLAN

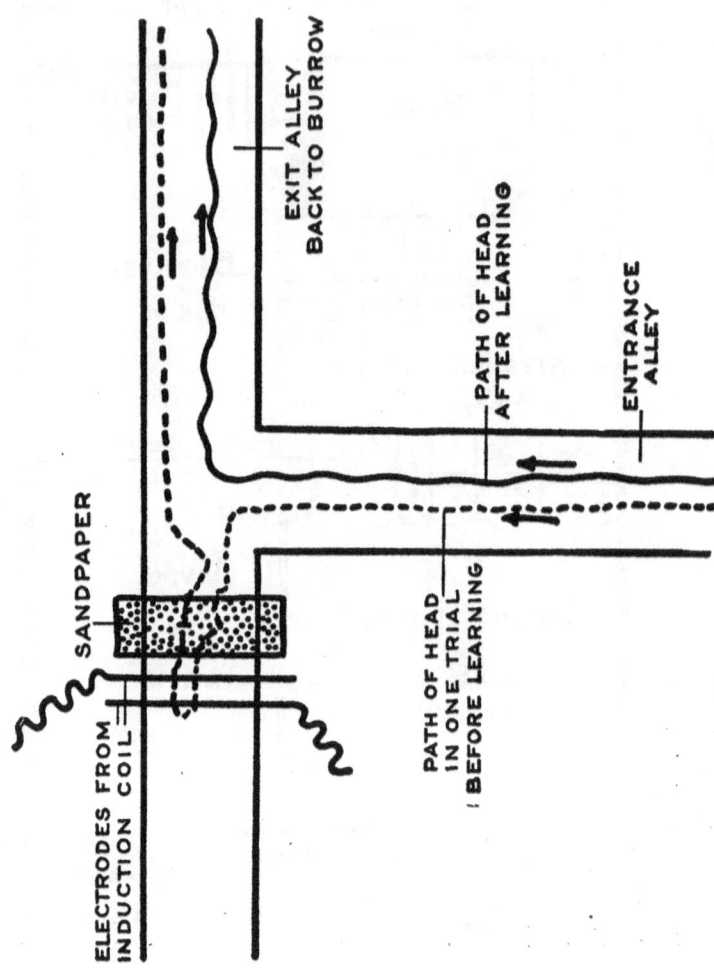

FIG. 94. EARTHWORM MAZE

Diagram of a type of earthworm maze devised by the authors as a modification of one described by Yerkes. By the use of this maze it is possible to study habit formation in the earthworm.

Steve Barbaro / *Space and Gesture*

being awakened in/ doors by/ a storm, one tends/ in haste to make/ sure of the fixity of
the world/

—and with the world one/ obsesses, but at least can make/ certain in the storm-
induced dark that the globes/ painted globes, the sort/ artisanal, even or/ not are not

spinning and spinning/ on the floors (unlike/ persons spinning doing/ so really only
for pleasure) covered with wet/ window shards/

—and surely a clinking or a jingling if
heard—if such rotation/ related noises persist, then the said/ *bearer* and hence

thinker often says/ I *must*/ *apply my* *still*/ *finger*, and so through touch/ gains
surety at/ the expense of movement

Douglas Basford / *Bore*

Call her a bore, if you like, or a boor,
but sound has a way of coercing sense
into bottlenecks worse than your parents
find late in the day driving to the Eastern Shore.

You'll hear about it later. You can be sure
images your mother half-absorbed—goldfinches,
drab bramble, wafer sun—will come. Clairaudience
of your eye, let's call it, keeps your eye turned

out the car window when the traffic's stock-still,
with nothing much to hear, no road noise, essence
of life distilled down to siblings squabbling
in a backseat ahead, to a few drunks stumbling
out past the shoulder and back. Something pinches
after you and misses. Reasons to speak dwindle.

Lindsay Bell / *Only Bends*

My heart is a hard metal object,
objet d'art, pointless, pointillist,
endowed with endless points,
pornographic, my heart is a hard-on,
she is the small descent into wild
idealism, my heart is a heavy
bauble exchanged with a merciful
friend on the sober end of a party;
my heart is on the drunk end,
an ear rubbed raw from watchwords
and sycophantic humping, who
convinces herself of the ethereal
merit of physical lack, my heart,
she is jealous, stays inside, pouts
that no one thought to call, can
afford good wine, but drinks sour,
my heart, she is a tiny fist, swings
with all the forethought and precision
of a trap, nicking a mouse's tail,
my heart, she is the cheese,
my heart, she stands alone.

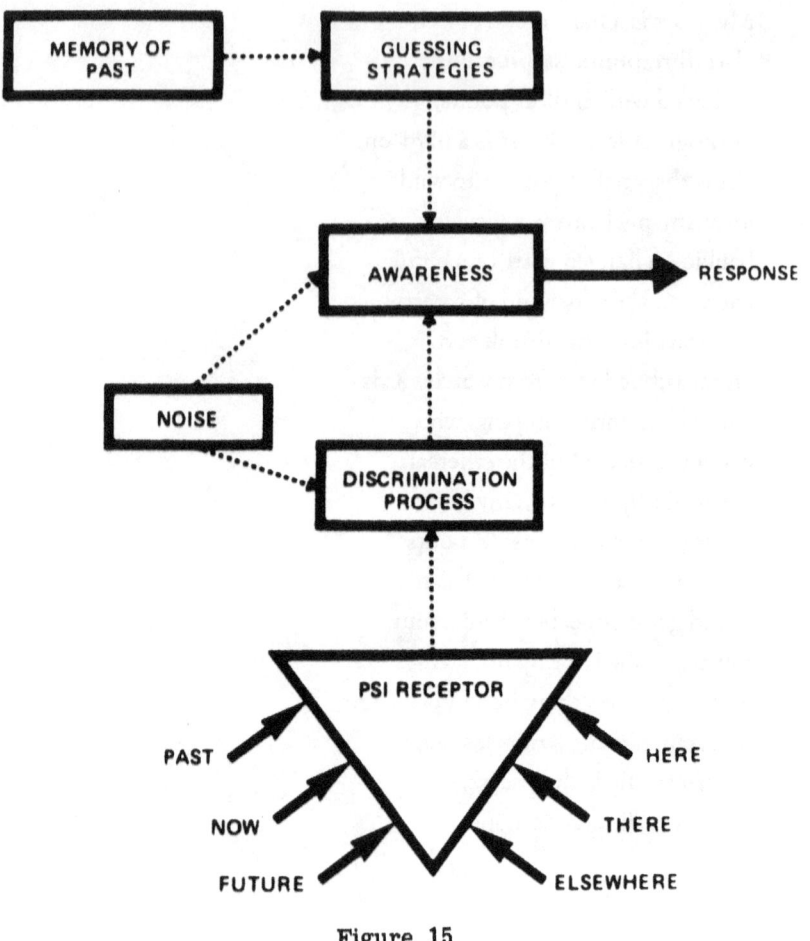

Figure 15

Samantha Bell / *Definitions: A Historical Approach*

Frippery: n. The clothing that I wear. The clothing that *we* wear. The clothing that is sold at the VOA in Brockport, NY on a rainy, dreadfully sunny day, crisp lines of strict sunbeam slanted across the pleated, outdated skirts, those pants the dressmaker once touched with golden fingers, flush with opportunity. Now, holes which Ben slowly traces, stuffs his fingers into, wonders if he should take them for five bucks even. The place where memories ache with lace burden, tremble with woolen recollection, flashes of business lunches and meetings downtown, all these clothes in our young hands, the register barely managing all the plans we have with them.

Looking glass: adj. My looking-glass self refigures my skinny image after I eat these French fries, my looking-glass self imagines I am obese, licking the pig fat from the bone leftover, my looking-glass self hinged on the hanger with the black bodice dress, slinky and a dream. My looking-glass self, imagined in black, imagined in silk, imagined in tiny dots of dizzy starvation, my looking-glass self a ghost in this window, the snow gray and loose around my looking-glass hips.

Malapropism: v. or n. "I am so incredibly kidnapped by your love!" I said to him, nervously, so calm and surprised and unreliable. His eyes gleamed like topaz squares, rubies in his Irish head, the freckles diseased and moving. "I wish I knew the future of that day, long ago!" I said, that moment, the sky bright with orange storm, the clouds stagnating in the offensive flurry of our new hearts, lifeless, fueling such heat between us. "Our love," I asked, menacingly, "is like this chicken wing, greasy and unspoken," and I held up the bony structure, boneless and chill, hot and spicy, mild and molded, clucking at how soft this new love was.

Photograph: v. When you photographed me, I was wedded to you. When you photographed me, I was wearing white. When you photographed me, I was on the green lawn, shivering in the hilly shadow of afternoon, the elm tree chill. When you photographed me, I was smiling, bright, when you photographed me, I was your bride and your joy. When you photographed me, I noticed and posed. When you photographed me, the air clasped my hand, the lake smoothed its surface, the layers of cake bent upon their morsels; when you photographed me, we were wed.

Pumpkin: n. My father buys a pumpkin for my seventh Halloween. He buys one that is perfectly round, carrot orange in its entire circumference. In the small kitchen, in our new cul-de-sac house, my father encourages me to cut through the gourd, to raise my stiff, scared elbow and "get right in there." With my orange pumpkin-knife, I slice through the layers, thick, and hit the slimy seeds. They seethe with anger, being so exposed. He pops the top off, lifts me up, lets me peer directly in; the orb is pulse and the orb is fresh. It is a field circumnavigating its way through One Knapps Circle. We plunge our hands, grasp at pulp, grind our teeth, until the world inside is flat and empty, void. Inside, later, he will light a tiny candle, and it will flicker, but the light inside will never be the same.

Vulture: n. On the side of the road sits a bird, bigger than I expected. His eyes are red and burning. His lips ache with prey. In front of him, beyond the pebbly black claws, a skunk, decaying each day on our nightly walk home, the stench a capable level of rot and dirt, a sequential step in the cycle. Photographed, the vulture would say, "I mean business," or, "I eat this now," but mostly, "I own this." He owns the lawn, where, just beyond, a tidy Sorority House stands with pink banners, held with wire and bow. A bird: an animal: Diclofenac will kill him before it kills cows; he ingests anything that can possibly decay. A systematic reconciliation with the world: a mercy, someone to remove the messy evidence of plausible suffering.

Knife: v. When my father called, far away from me, a plane ride away over lakes in the Minnesota landscape, across icy fields, his suicidal high notes took over most of the conversation. My voice couldn't rise over the diagnosis, the incessant declarative bang of a mental disease, as big as any crevasse after someone has fallen through. His voice spliced each careful, sliced syllable, dicing and knifing through *threat, myself,* and *mania,* cuts as dewy red as paper over a diligent finger on a July Monday morning. Knifed and diced, his entire history, something cutting bone, something black and alien, coarse and dense. Ahistorically, he knifed through me.

Blunt: adj. My mother had naturally blonde hair, naturally great big blue eyes, naturally she said things like, "If you have nothing nice to say, say nothing at all." At night, she wrapped her delicate pearl fingers around a crisp gin, a crisp tonic, condensation glowering in the loose dusk. To my father, at night, the real lessons: "Go to hell," and "You asshole," and "I hate you." These signatures, like graffiti on a cold stone wall, blunt and drone, slick with worry, almost but not quite right.

Blunt: n. The night: thick. The car: smoke. The day: gone. Wu-Tang blaring in the backseat, the seats rumbling, a man I think I love, from college, from this town I visit him in, from the streets sliding by, a blunt in two small hands, brown, disheveled, strong. The drug fits between my lips, caresses the lengths of time between here and there, between mom and dad, between girl and boy. The street lights flaunt sober joy, careful purpose, direction. In quietude, later, I know I do not love him, I know I cannot love him, I know I cannot say it, I know I cannot say it, I know I do not love him; I do not know how to be blunt.

Magnificent: adj. My father walked the dog on the canal path in winter. The trees nestled on the eroding edges, the soft pallid snow rested on the branches. The dog's feet made a path in the snow. The trees sometimes made an arch, and he would stop. He put his hands behind his back, acquitting something like guilt for these small, cold moments. The dog would walk far from him, sunspots colliding on her back and her paws. Her ears flapped a dense, sensible brown, loyal to gravity.

She got far away each time, his brown eyes would flicker, and panic, the trees a mess of nuisance, a blip in the line of sight. He would call her name, and she would come. The sun would converge on the tops of their heads, the precise hue of the dirt underfoot. Their steps evident in the bedded snow; their voices, calm, in the gaining distance.

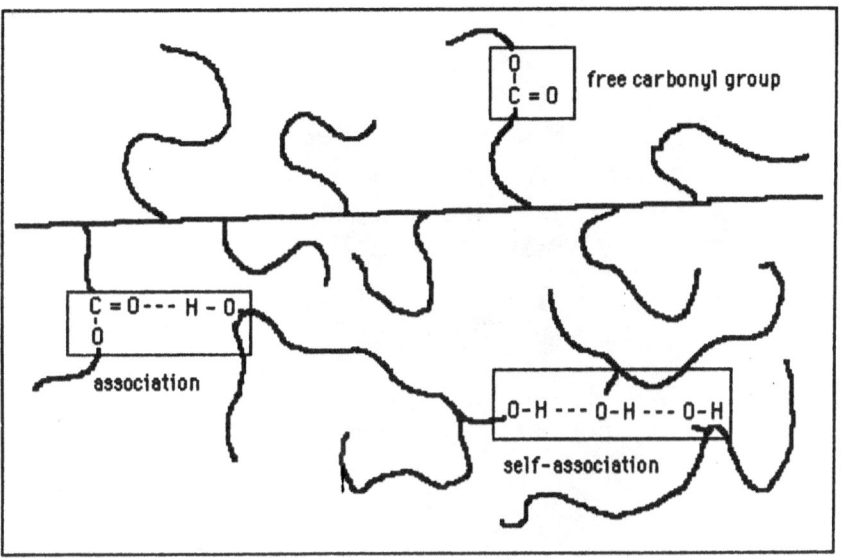

Fig. 4.   Illustration of the types of hydrogen bonds present in blends of rigid rods with ester groups on the side chains and random coils with hydroxyl groups.

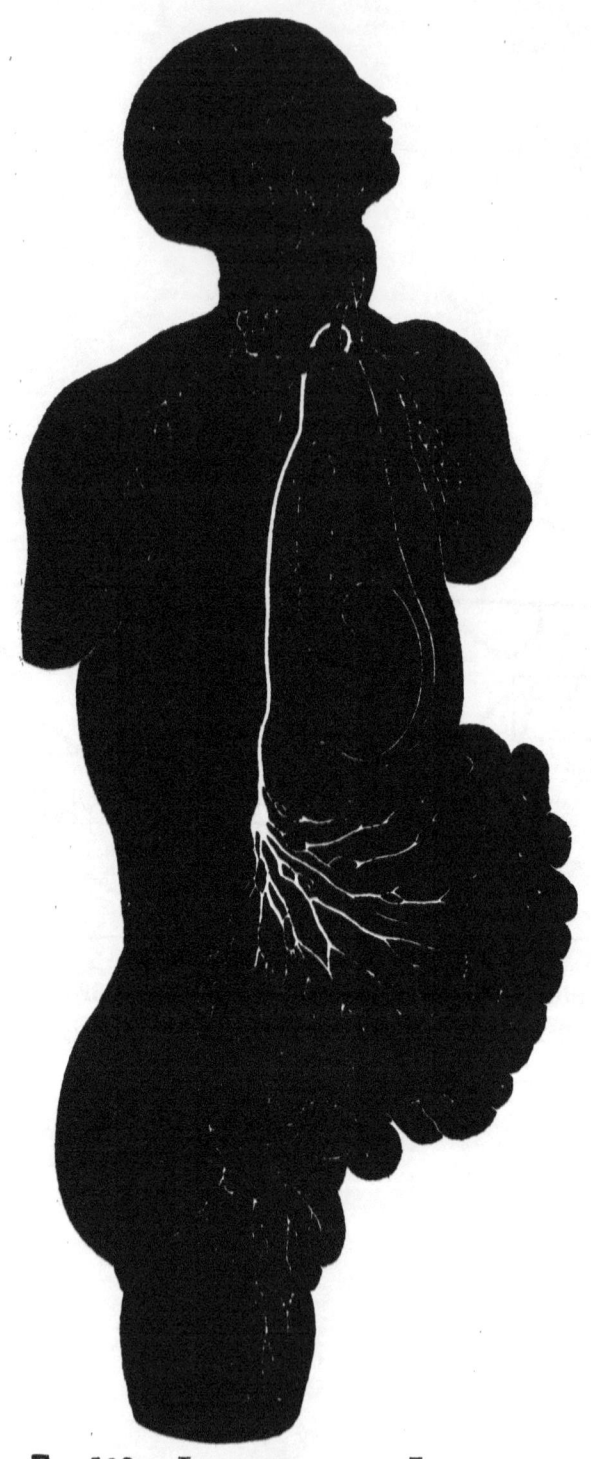

FIG. 193. LACTEALS AND LYMPHAT-
ICS, DURING DIGESTION.

Elisabeth Benjamin / *Her Slideshow*

My sister leaves our house early; I watch her through my window. Before sunrise, I hear the door slam, and I'm up. Likely, she has waded into the pond, which she calls the lake, and she is naked because she thinks I'm sleeping. Through blue light I see her move away from the house. I get back in bed and dream of the next two days. Everything will be gone then.

My sister eats the leaves when she's done drinking tea. She saves them for last to be spooned out, like dessert. If her tea goes cold, she heats it on the stove, then drinks until it goes cold again. She doesn't strain out the tealeaves, and this is something that bothers me. She doesn't tell my fortune in the dregs, nor does she read her own. She just eats them.

My sister's body is like mine stretched out. Hipbones jut out, caging in her stomach. Shoulders round knobs, arms drip down into frond fingers. She has two inches on me, something worth quarreling about, though we should be past the age of quarreling about degrees of tallness, or of shortness in my case. As we grew she surpassed me, her long limbs and her natural wit. She became our parents' favorite girl, the pretty one, the spirited one.

My sister refuses to ask me to stay. Tomorrow I am moving from this house of ours. In the end, she will say Good Riddance, or Scram. The rain will greet me as I leave the house, and she will wait until I'm down the road before she strips and runs into the water. I'll hear the splash and keep walking. She wishes there were waves in the water, tides, but it's only a green pond.

My sister collects slides and projects them onto the living room wall. Vacationing families we've never met build sand castles and sleep open-mouthed in hammocks. We sightsee at another's safari, when we've never been to a zoo. Monochromatic lions loll in her stills, and we feel like part of it all. There are slides in our attic, of our family, but my sister isn't interested in those.

My sister is bored by laps, so she mostly moves in small circles, or she just splashes around a lot. She floats face down, looking for fish. She floats on her back, her feet slowly kicking to prevent her lower body from sinking. I'd like to see her from underwater, her cropped hair splayed out on the surface. I'd like to see the notches in her spine, have access to the vulnerability of a turned back.

My sister is concerned with color. "Ochre has outshone sepia," she says solemnly one morning over toast and butter, over eggs and applesauce, over oatmeal. She wears red and says, "Read my red," and I am to understand her temperament. She consumes color carefully: red-stalked chard, blueberries, pink grapefruit, golden mirabelles, rare meats, gelatin in primary colors.

My sister and I share familial features. I see the resemblances: the narrow faces and round eyes and straight long noses. Our bones are the same, but she wears her flesh right. She grows threads of golden hair. Something makes her delicately beautiful and me ordinary. She walks like she knows people. It's a combination of the things she is and the things I can't be, like I could never be a snail or leaves. I could never be like her.

My sister destroys this house our father built in anticipation of us. There are two bedrooms, theirs and ours, but I moved into their room after they left us. After we drove them away. When the roof needs fixing, or the house needs painting, my sister and I do the work ourselves. We contend with termites and storms. Raccoons tore off the gutters last year trying to take refuge from winter in our attic.

My sister asks, "Why are you leaving?" and I say, "I am too old for this funhouse." I tug at the puppy-print curtains. I'm sick of spectacles. Leaving for my room, I kick through mangled toys, torn books, dented kettles, broken glass, buttons. My room bears deliberate cleanliness. The rest of the house is my sister's: the bathroom where our mother once dipped locks of our hair in warm water and rolled them up in old baby socks, the muddy cellar.

My sister is twenty-three and I am twenty-six. For years I was her pleasant paper doll. She dressed me up and colored my face with oil pastels. With pinned lengths of fabric, she wrapped my shapeless body into something unrecognizable. She agreed with my compliance and silence, and then I grew up and became an unruly plaything. I ripped through seams and tugged at pins until she despised me.

My sister says, "Your assortment of browns has prolonged fall unnecessarily. You insist on honoring the dying, on disturbing nature and its seasons." I look down at my shades of browns, which match my hair and freckled skin. She's right: I'm drab and depressing to look at, but we rarely leave our property anymore. She acts as if the chickens are disapproving of my creased plainness, while applauding her unkempt grace.

My sister hears me say, "Would you like to make slides from our adventures?" but she stares silently at the wall's landscape. "I can take pictures as you ride your bike into the pond," I say. She says, "That's not an adventure. We have never been on an adventure." I ask her what she would call tight-rope walking, or squirrel catching, or squid hacking, and she says, "Boring." Glancing up at me, she flinches with what I understand as contempt.

My sister drapes herself with antique jewelry, our mother's forsaken bangles, things from our grandmother's trunk. She dumps out the tackle boxes and clips the barbs off of our father's flashiest fishing lures, fashioning gruesome broaches. She scales herself in sparkles, fastening anything shiny to herself. Swathes of sequins and shards of colored glass pile up. She is a tropical fish; I am a shipwreck.

My sister makes decisions based on how things look. Once I saw a man kiss her, so deeply, like he was drinking from a well of nectar, like the thirstiest man in the world. I was up in the window again; they were on the front walk. As he kissed her, she went limp, her eyes open and lazy, bored during her first kiss. She came into the house humming a slow sad song. We have so few interactions with outsiders.

My sister eats small servings off of saucers. I say, "The saucers are for the teacups," and she smashes a saucer on the floor. Bits of our mother's abandoned porcelain dance into the corners of the kitchen. Whatever she eats, little cairns of sunflower seeds and raisins, sticks to the bottoms of our shoes and leaves the floor that way. We track them outside and into our beds and the hamper. They eventually disappear; I sweep up the saucer remains a few months later.

My sister won't ask where I'm going. But if she did, I would tell her this: "I'm leaving this place for somewhere by the sea." If she asks where I got the money, I will say, "Mom and Dad sent it to me and said to keep it from you." These are both lies; she will recognize them. I don't have money to get to the seashore, and we haven't heard from our parents since we were teenagers. But they're the only soft spot left, for me at least.

My sister and I were fifteen and eighteen when our parents disappeared. The day before I had planned a successful attack, one in a series of jokes, trapping our mother in the cellar with her rainbow of preserves. My sister was the one to keep the door closed for too long; our father came home and released his wife. They took very little with them, probably only a suitcase each. They fled from this house and from us.

My sister runs from the house to the pond in her birthday suit, and I forget what kind of a person she is. She's the kind of person who licks the last cupcake but won't eat it. Who pitches the last jar of preserves off the roof, just to hear the sound of breaking. Who kicks hens. My sister is wonderful and despicable. I love her, but I lock my bedroom door at night.

My sister's name is Gretchen, and mine is Robin. Our names aren't used much because we've been the only ones here for so long. There's no confusion about who we're addressing because there's no one here but us. I sometimes write her little notes, and she scratches through her name, writing 'you' above it. She hasn't spoken my name in years; however, she greets the birds outside, calling them all robins regardless of species.

My sister is wet and holding something. By the sink, I'm washing my traveling clothes. Her hand clenched tight and dripping, she plunges her fist into the laundry water. We watch black tendrils seep out between her fingers. The water turns gray and opaque and my clothes gather sediment. She strolls out the back door and I see her dive off the dock into the pond. Surfacing, she has one arm in the air, black scum dripping down her wiry arm.

My sister hasn't mentioned my packing. I'm taking the medium-sized leather case from the attic. The leather is damaged from moisture and dust, so I'll spend part of the day seasoning it with oil from the kitchen. I'm packing some clothes and a few books. No trinkets, memorabilia, or items laden with nostalgia. My sister and I are not sentimental people.

My sister's antics demand difficult decisions. As she heads back toward the house, I think: Shall I lock the door and watch as she smears a handful of muck down the window? She will make the most horrible face at me, a face that says, Why are you doing this to me? and I'll open the door for her and face her wrath. Or I let her continue filling the sink with mud, soiling my best clothes, until I have nothing nice to pack. I sit at the kitchen table and wait it out.

My sister doesn't find me interesting, and I think she's crazy. She clips her toenails while I'm in the room. She exhales audibly as I am enjoying the quiet. She paces over creaky floorboards. When she says a little bit, she means a lot. My sister circles her bruises in ballpoint pen. She pokes my bruises with a long finger. In the two weeks she's known that I'm leaving, she has not asked where I'm going.

My sister likes nothing more than a brick wall behind a window. She saw a photograph of this once in an old magazine. The wood frame exposing nothing. A glassless, lightless window to nowhere at all. She places empty picture frames on the wall to simulate a bricky window. "What's that?" I say. "Oh, that's a picture of our wallpaper," she says, then she laughs herself sick. Each room has these vacant frames.

My sister swims. I watch her catch fish with our father's old pole. She throws the small ones over the little embankment, something she read about controlling the population and the size. Maybe we'll have catfish for dinner. Bare-footed, mud-slippered, she comes into the kitchen and slaps a few fish onto the counter. They're still flopping and I take an ice pick to their brains. I gut them into the sink. My sister watches but doesn't help.

My sister and I live on twenty acres of fruit trees. I keep a garden in the summer, and I can whatever we have left. I can cherries and tomatoes and strawberries and pears. We sell peaches. She doesn't help with the garden, but she tends to our chickens because she likes them personally. If she didn't feel that way about them, she would neglect them completely, like cleaning or combing her hair or our parents.

My sister is long and lovely, but she would not be nearly so lovely if I didn't care for her. I trim her hair and wash her clothes. She likes having her hair tugged, so I lace my fingers through her tangles and I cup her scalp and tug. Harder, she says, but it always feels like her roots will give out, and I ease up. I give her a short spiky cut because she's like an unruly child.

My sister tires of filling the sink with mud. I draw a new basin of water and rewash my things. She stands outside watching me through the window. I study her face, her nose lightly touching the glass. I see no remorse. These staring contests, trying to see ourselves in the other sister, I will miss. Right now, in her face I see nothing. Not our mother, not myself. It's just a face, which will blink soon, which will turn and move toward the pond.

My sister built a brick wall over the window of the downstairs bathroom. Days of hauling bricks and mixing cement and slapping them together like so many lopsided sandwiches. The project brought her many hours of good spirits. She wore yellow for days afterward, indicating general cheerfulness. We keep the pale blue lace curtains over the window, which she says increase the magnificence of the brick-walled window.

My sister and I celebrated our liberation from parents. I disguised my sadness with whoops and streamers; we marched around the property waving our underwear on broom handles. We considered ourselves castaways, victims of providential mutiny. My sister draped the house in colorful fabrics, covering pictures, the piano, chandeliers. I baked cherry pies for dinner. Now we use our father's shirts as dust cloths. I sold most of our mother's things.

My sister swims early, then comes in and flips on the projector. The couch holds her wetness like a shadow. She curls up in the same spot, next to the projector and the box of slides. She moves slowly, taking time to memorize scenes and faces. I come down to find her in her towel and I sit close to her. I lean in and sometimes she puts her head on my shoulder. I know if I move she'll get up, so I breathe slowly and quietly. Soon, we eat oatmeal and sausage.

My sister only cares for summer. She swims past fall and ends up with an annual November chest cold, which signifies winter. In winter she walks on ice. We've lived here so long, but memories of winter are always erased by warm months. In winter my sister can't get warm. I ache watching her shiver, but I can't get her to bundle up. I never remember what we eat or when we sleep in winter: It's all summers around here.

My sister has a star-shaped scar on her wrist, the size of a penny. It's a foggy white stain over blue veins. She bends her hand back, stretching the skin of her wrist, and admires her star. I don't understand such homage paid to an old wound, but I guess it might be different if I had a star shape to remember. I wonder if she knows its origin, the little scrape that came from the dock, the infection, the picking. I bet she doesn't remember.

My sister scatters her chickens. She tries leashing one to thin rope; she tries to walk chickens to town. In town they stare at us. My sister is disheveled, but mostly we look like regular people. Once, when asked the whereabouts of our parents, my sister said, "We hated them so much that they vanished." As she said this she demonstrated their disappearance by slowly drawing together her thumb and pointer, the pads of her fingers pinched tight, like: Poof!

My sister and I gig frogs around the perimeter of the pond. Frogging. With headlamps and stakes we stalk and stab, mercilessly. When I get a frog, I hand its twisted body to my sister, she removes its legs and adds them to her collection. She wears a wicker basket at her hip. It's brutal business, but it's dark. She will cook them up the way our father used to. This is the only cooking she does. I doubt she'll cook anything once I'm gone.

My sister and I have the same birthday. This unlikely probability caused many childhood quarrels, but now we've resolved to an unspoken treaty of forgetful, birthdayless years, which is better than aging anyway. However, this year I found in an antique shop in town a box of old slides, decades of a family's memories, three continents, four births, two new houses and a death. She kicked me for not telling her it was our birthdays, but she loved the gift.

My sister's star-shaped scar, wrists, her dry, gray elbows. My sister's cropped gold hair, her pink scalp exposed. She refuses to wear sun block. She shuns block. Constantly shedding, her pink skin peels layer after layer, until all that's left is thin brown limbs, taut polished bends, cheekbones. I ask so little. I'm always telling her to brush her teeth, like a child she must be reminded. I'm tired of telling her.

My sister hates her name because it's Gretchen. When we were children, she would curse our parents for naming her something so ugly. I would say it was our grandmother's name, and Gretchen would say, "Our grandmother was a hag," even though we never met her. Hers is a face scratched off of family pictures. My sister's name is elegant and classic. A Robin is a plain bird, especially a female robin, which is small and brown. Gretchen means little pearl.

My sister sits on my bed in a rare moment as I fold clothes and stack them in my suitcase. She watches me but when I glance up, she pretends to look out the dark window. She says, "Do you wish they had stayed?" and I have no answer for her. She's asking if I blame her and if that's why I'm going. I imagine her asking if she can join me tomorrow, and I imagine telling her no. She's sitting still, waiting for an answer that I will not give.

My sister ignores me for days after I tell her. We eat separately and she swims while I make lists of things to do before I leave. From the desk in my room I can see her; she consciously manipulates shadows, her eyes to surfaces. It's too bright out for her to look at anything else, so she watches shadows as intently as her slides. Later she swims, eyes closed, feeling the heat, seeing red through her eyelids, knowing I'm in the window watching.

My sister's lovely. I am a robin living with a pearl, and birds like sparkles. She tells me to leave her alone, to stop picking. She tells me she's an adult. She says, "I can take care of my own teeth," except she doesn't. Some- times she leaves in the morning and doesn't return until after dark. I don't mention it, but I wonder where she goes. I picture her sleeping in trees, digging, chasing animals. I wonder what she's hidden.

My sister scratches our family out of old slides. She says familiar im- ages are useless. With a penknife she scrapes at them, carving a void into pictures of the farm. Empty tree swings. Vacant canoes. Mystery shoes. I worry about my sister. I'm accustomed to her behavior, but our parents found it alarming. But, they left me too, both of us. There's something about me they wanted to leave behind. I wasn't in on their escape.

My sister will behave as if I never existed. I'll hear the splash on my way out, and the instant she hits the water, she'll forget, like she forgot our parents. As if our mother never painted her nails pink. As if our father never sang songs or fried fish. We all played jacks together, raced across the pond, cupped lightning bugs and left them in glass jars—later in wood and mesh boxes built by our father. When I leave it will be like this, this forgetting.

My sister has gone to bed later than usual after watching me pack. Perhaps she wanted to be near me some my last night here. She probably thinks I'll never visit. Knowing she's asleep helps me think. I don't know where I'm going tomorrow; I just know it's time to leave. It's almost fall, and I'm almost twenty-seven. In the morning I will kiss her on the forehead, the way our mother did, then I'll walk to the train station, see where it's going and go.

My sister's hair, tangled, matted, hopeless. I wish I had pictures of it all. Of her swimming through blue light, through fog. Nothing will be left tomorrow, this house is ours. It was never our parents'; he built it in anticipation of us. Maybe this was their plan all along. I would project them on the wall of wherever I end up. Mother's confusion and dark lips, father's plaid, the garden. Gretchen pressed against the window, staring in at me.

My sister has filled the sink, handful by handful, with muck that has displaced soapy water. Water overflows onto the wood floor. My sister's picture frame installation is a tribute to our parents, as if the pictures' inhabitants fled along with them. My sister slides her hand under a frame and waves at me through space. She fills the sink, and this will prevent me from leaving? My sister refuses to ask me to stay, to ask me where I'm going.

My sister leaves. It's morning and I'm searching for her. I'm trying to say goodbye. As I go downstairs, I hear the purr of the slide projector, and I expect to find her warming her fine hands over its humming heat. She's gone, of course. I search the house, the pond, the shed for her. I turn her room inside out. No note, no trace of a departure, just a black and white image of Honolulu on the wall. My suitcase floats in the pond, the remnant of castaway sisters.

Ash Bowen / *Albert Goldbarth's MFA Thesis*

must have been genius. But I like
to think of Goldbarth before all that:
his Iowa writing room, the dog-eared pages
of everything—*Popular Mechanics*,
Poetry, Scientific American, maybe
Monarch Notes for whatever
wasn't available. In the corner,
a space robot with killer pinchers,
a soft disposition and a heart
that pumped Plutonium-239, the isotope
the Manhattan Project liked to play with.

Night and day, Goldbarth lumbering
through his room of radioactive dust,
his black-rimmed glasses blurred
by atomic fallout, his eyes spiraling
like a B-movie hypnotism screen—
that's Goldbarth to me. Goldbarth
in the quad. Goldbarth out for coffee.
Goldbarth shot down by girls in a bar.
The real Goldbarth. Before awards
made Goldbarth Goldbarth, when
he was alone in his room, just
waiting for a carcinogenic machine
to cough him the next line.

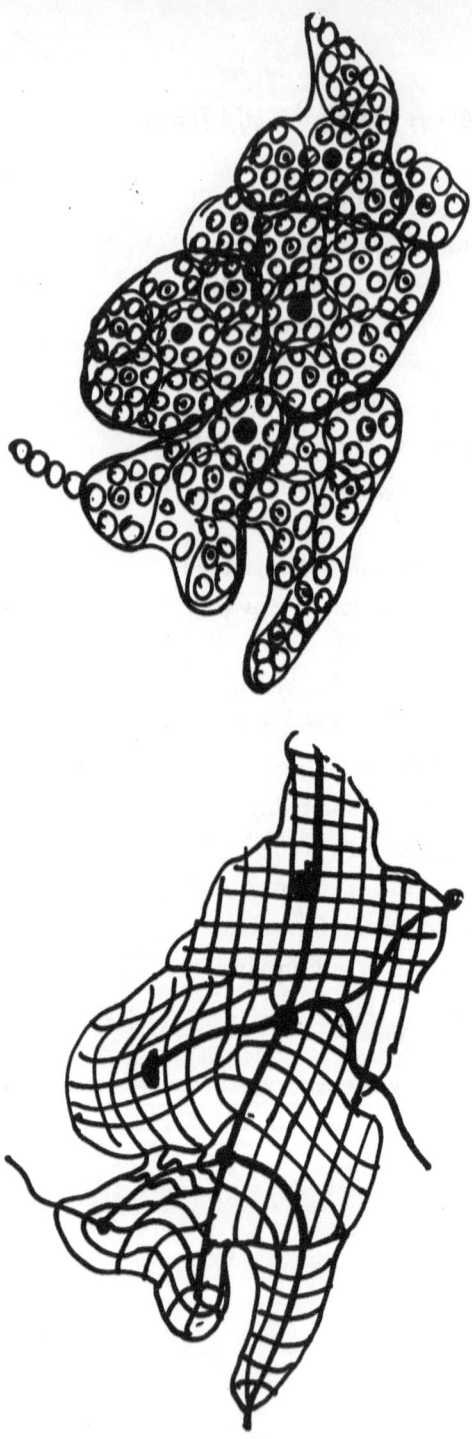

The ecumenopolis, or universal city,
which Dr. Doxiadis envisions will have all networks
of transportation and utilities buried in
the ground and interconnecting with communities
as in the grid structure at bottom. Upon this
structural framework, cities and urban regions will
merge and blend with a texture shown at top.
Instead of being in conflict with the machine, man
will be free to move and develop himself.

Jason Bredle / *Spontaneous Overflow of Emotion Recollected in the Sea of Tranquility*

Lately my dreams have been haunted by penises. Never before have I stood on the shores of so many seas and felt so empty. I miss your hair. How are the cherry blossoms? Describe to me the spring rain. I'm sad my cricket died. I've replaced him with a basketball I named Spalding after Spalding Gray. I saw something like this in a movie once and it seemed like a good idea. As you may imagine, Spalding and I have many, many lively discussions on a variety of interesting topics well into the night. Masturbating in one sixth the gravity of earth is fun. It feels crazy when I ejaculate. I miss your cooking. I want a Dr. Pepper. I want to play catch with a child. When I close my eyes all I see are butterflies. When I close my eyes all I see are strawberries. That shaking my hands do? It's getting worse. If I tell you something, will you promise not to tell anyone? Love is a wet helmet. This is all an elaborate way of saying I hate camping. I can feel it. I'm on the verge of a psychological breakthrough.

The Club

I read something upsetting in a magazine. One season I ate a spoonful of salt and butter every morning at 10:00. The sports team I supported was suspended on allegations of cheating. My father was miserable but acted as if he wasn't miserable. We'd climb the fence, play tennis and swim in the country club pool after dark. It turned out he was drunk but I didn't know it. In retrospect, it was the 90's and the guy was still playing with a wooden racket. There are many clubs you could join. In some you're spanked and in others you're brainwashed through torture then loosed upon the earth. I like when someone offers me a meal and a place to stay if I'm ever in Penang. I'm going to be so late because I have to stop at a bookstore and pick up a gigantic coffee table book of old maps. In Spanish they call a club sandwich a "club sandwich." I wrote this, lost it, then rewrote it from the memory of having written it. What do you think so far?

The Book of Evil

There's a guy out there who likes to dangle his genitals in his aquarium.
I like butterscotch pudding. It's true I've dibble dabbled in the occult
philosophies. Here's a mantra: go out, go wild and do it again and again.
Out there conversations about model rocketry dissolve into the night.
You talk until you question how you ever got into this conversation about
what kind of job you can do with no hands. I have some personal issues
I really need to deal with at the moment. When there's music I make up
little dances to do with the neighbor's cat. I appreciate that the cat toler-
ates them. Did a disembodied voice just insult my maturity? I think we're
in trouble because the cat spends more and more time pacing and looking
at me as if waiting for me to do something. I'm on the couch bombarding
myself with incredible scents. I wish I could drink from the fountain of
forgetfulness. We're running out of places to hide. We'll have to leave for
another place soon. I don't want to go to that place because there's a book
of evil buried there.

The Carnival

You forget so much and it makes me sad. I like holding your hand on
the ferris wheel because it makes you happy. There's one little dude in
the Gravitron. A girl with a bloody nose is escorted from the Himalaya.
Tell me, do you like corndogs? What about onion rings? I had something
funny to tell you but I can't remember what it was. I'm committed to liv-
ing and dying in the fast lane. I want to lose my wallet on the Hellbender
while the operator enjoys a fried chicken dinner with a side of baked beans
and cole slaw. I want to win an enormous stuffed pig and save the lives of
hundreds of goldfish. Everywhere there are lights and music and children
with blue lips. Have you ever wondered what it's like to bury yourself in
candy? I'm a little paranoid. If only I knew that in a few months we'll never
speak again. Now's the time to celebrate. You wear white all week, you
wear red all weekend. After I die, I want my friends to take my corpse to
all my favorite places. I want them to begin at the carnival.

Nickole Brown / *St. Michael of Valu-Mart*

Lift your light. Lift your two dollar ten cent light to us, Señor De Los Angeles, your crayon red gel candle, your sticker with sword and scales and black demon under your gold-sandaled feet, Michael, a painted circa 1975 Michael, looking like a Ken doll in Rome.

Lift the light we just lit, Michael, ceremoniously with a Zippo, Michael, because even the poor need ceremony, the candle burning dangerously close to dingy sheets and braided legs and wide, wild hair.

Michael, show us which way, all this yearning for one another, show us the way

through the cathedral, we've never been, Michael, churches you know so well, we're waiting to enter from outside, show us how to tolerate the snow, our tennis shoes not made for winter, such slippery ice, such a stone path, the hostas dormant, the stars stark. Pretend we are choirboys, Michael, castrated sopranos for you, our throats bared for you, and it is our job to make Christmas mass beautiful.

We are shielding the light, Michael, our boyhands cup the flame and our thin, flammable choir robes blow, frankincense smoke swinging ahead. Won't you let us in?

Lift it, Michael, we are lost, we are poor, we don't know better. Rest your tired heel, Michael, the barracuda is dead, it is crushed on the pier, hook still in its mouth. Bed down

with us, Michael, it is time to rest, because all of this: the sheets, the snow, the smoke, the fish, its blood, all of this is in the taste of our mouths, our tongues pressed to your pretty feet in prayer.

Some Facts About a Cow

Her breathing is winged and deep. If she lets you, put your hand over the fence to her nose to feel the cannon-sized ball of air in your palm. If not, stand back and listen. With your eyes closed, that exhale could belong to a dolphin swimming alongside your boat, the slick gray spout opening with a burst of spray.

She could live to be fifteen, but she'll be slaughtered by two after reaching about 1,200 pounds, just the right size to fit her marbled flesh perfectly inside a box to be stamped with a blue stamp and shipped across a blue sea.

She must give birth before she gives milk, but don't worry: the farmers are good Jews. Even Christ's cup and plate were separate vessels passed around the table, keeping the body we eat and the body we drink from segregated and holy.

From her gelatin, we get photographic film. Imagine: we take a snapshot of a dolphin breathing, the fin cresting the same waves where the shipment of her flesh floats and sways.

Under a full moon, her white face floats like a ghost. Her head, decapitated by the dark, is an insomniac of cud and chew, ceaselessly worrying the grass. If she knows little of the expanse of this field and nothing of time, why? She cannot chew enough.

Her tongue is cat-scratch dry, salt-searching, scared. A farmer tells you she prefers wet grass, *to make washing it down that much easier,* and you think of sacrifice, how humbly she drinks the rain.

Stephen Burt / *Over Connecticut: Eminent Domain*

Inland, the antique milemarkers spread
themselves out into twentieth-century lanes,

jammed up this afternoon, though built for speed—
sun-harmed, old news, old toys, they bury the lead

of Prudence Crandall's schoolroom heritage,
her kettle of cider, her wishes traced by hand.

We miss her now. We parcel out her land.
Town halls fade into greenery like spies.

New London's keeping Groton in its sights;
its drawbridge swings, a military career.

New Haven is old scores and old concrete,
old freeways where the Great Migration stalled;

the Sound turns agate, band by frozen band.
By Haddam, there are only Linens-n-Things

and other things, great mounds, whole civilizations
still glowing in faint spits along Route Nine…

I miss the Great Society with its sense
that we could redraw maps that ailed us, gone

in a mist of real estate and demonstrations,
three or four angry years before I was born.

Oxo Vegetable Peeler

Its mission is not to reveal any one fact or facet, but simply to keep the investigation going, line by line, until some oblong or oblate gets worn enough to take what we recognize as its shape. There are fleshes within each flesh, a core in each core.

Does the peeler know, as it exercises the powers inherent in its metal edge, how with just a little more push or perspicuity it could simply continue, strip after strip, making spirals around a single and continuously diminishing rind or skin, until the entirety of an object lies discarded in the sink, like an abstract proposition disproved? The peeler continues, so easily held…so much we attribute, wrongly, to one human hand.

Blake Butler / *Insomnia Door*

1. Every moment that I sleep I've fought for with my entire body.
2. God still insists on waking me up every other hour.
3. Every other every other hour I am compelled to stumble to the restroom.
4. I believe I have the same size bladder I did at age eight.
5. If it's not the matter of a small bladder, there's a chance I have prostate cancer.
6. I should probably see a doctor.
7. At age 27 I weigh eighty pounds less than I did the year I got my learner's.
8. I experienced fat terror from age ten to almost seventeen.
9. Husky is the preferred term for fat kids but still not something you want to hear.
10. Once at a car show with my parents an MC called me on stage to play along in his joke routine. He asked the question 'What do you do for fun?' and as he leaned down so I could speak into the microphone, he whispered a suggestion: 'Eat.'
11. I said 'Eat' into the microphone.
12. The audience cackled wildly.
13. Afterwards my mother asked me why I'd said it. I said I didn't know.
14. Afterwards also the MC gave me a free T-shirt: 'The Heartbeat of America: Today's Chevy Truck.'
15. The shirt was XXL.
16. I slept in it for years.
17. I slept so much better as a fat child.
18. Better sleep then often the result of having eaten an entire box of cereal before bed.
19. Perhaps surprisingly, the cereal in question was most often Crispix or Rice Chex, and 2%, not skim or whole.
20. I imagine this procedure is still effective for inducing drowsiness at age 27, though my stomach's no longer up for it.

21. I still get big kicks though from buying sub par synthetic sugar cereals such as Waffle-O's and Mini-Swirlz.

22. Bad sugar fuels fucked dreams.

23. Constantly recurring dream as a very young child in which I lay paralyzed in my bed, an enormous boulder lodged in the ceiling and rolling toward me in slow motion.

24. Always waking with the boulder just inches from my face.

25. Further research revealing this state was most likely hypnopompia: an intermediate consciousness occurring during waking.

26. Consciousness in which hallucination and sensing *a presence* are common.

27. What presence; when what where; who what this thing lodged in my ceiling.

28. Also associated with this phenomenon: alien abduction, telepathy, apparition and prophetic vision.

29. Often having slept with my head hung in the hallway so as to see my parents in the living room, fearing the presence.

30. Even just my mother's voice a comfort.

31. Though often also: sleep walking; sleep terror; talking in sleep; sleep sound.

32. More active maybe in my sleep than I often am in waking.

33. Perhaps infused within my blood.

34. A cousin once having woken with the front door to his house wide open, knowing he'd gone out.

35. *If the walker commits a criminal offence while asleep, the defence of automatism may be available.*

36. [List item 36 deleted for fear of repercussion.]

37. My sleep speech probably more exactly what I mean.

38. The dream me a clearer me.

39. Last night the real you having moved the dream me from my sofa to my bed.

40. Last night the real me having thrown a candy bar in frustration.

41. Never again, if anything, taking my fury out on candy.

42. Candy my one irrefutable, perfect lover.

43. Whose breasts and brains will never malform.

44. Who would wait forever by my deathbed, regardless.

45. Candy marriage still not legal in 50 of 50 American states.

46. Also not legally possible: marriage to one's dream self.

47. The becoming of one's dream self.

48. Willful confinement to the hypnopompic state.

49. The boulder above me, still proceeding.

50. My mom forever just down the hall.

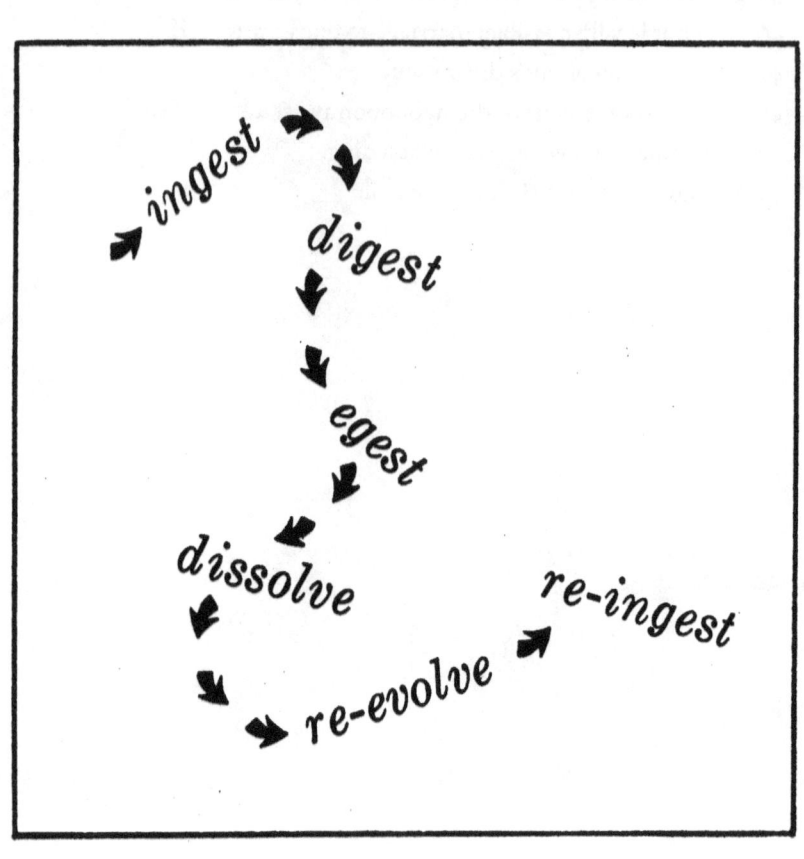

Edmond Caldwell / *A Shorter Organon of the New Science*

1.

What, another book on the brain? She's crazy for them, for these books
on the brain. It seems like every week there's a new book on the brain,
some of them even on the best-sellers list. Outside on the power line a
single crow shifts from claw to claw, as if the wire were too cold, unless
it is too hot. But its feathers are not puffed, the sign of a cold bird, and
the wire appears to be fully insulated. A "hot wire" is a stripped wire or a
loose wire, and this wire is fully-insulated and taut. Still the crow shifts, in
anticipation perhaps of the impending day, not long now, when absolutely
everything will be wireless. The crow has a bird brain, and yet crows are
reputed to be among the brainy birds, along with parrots and cockatoos.
There was a scientist who trained her cockatoo to learn up to eighty
words, pecking them out on a kind of keyboard with a pictograph for each
word. The cockatoo's favorite show was Sesame Street. The cockatoos are
among the long-lived birds, and yet this cockatoo never outgrew Sesame
Street, before it died. The crow on the power-line outside the window
dimly anticipates the impending day of complete wirelessness, a day
whose dawn is already at hand, or at claw, or as it were on the wing, a day
destined to bring with it not only complete wirelessness but the melting of
the polar ice caps, such that the land will be completely submerged in the
sea, to the advantage perhaps of the less-brainy seagull but to the disad-
vantage of crows. There will be no land to land on but there will be no
wires to stand on either, or rather, as now, on which to shift from claw to
claw. With its bird-brain the crow addresses itself to this problem.

2.

There are stacks of brain books on the display tables of all the bookstore
chains and even on the shelves of the vanishing independent booksellers,
every week a new brain book and every one of them, it seems, she reads.

She is fully up on the brain. Research on the brain, or brain science, is being done all over the country, behind the walls of medical centers and universities all over the country, but the best thinking about the brain and certainly the best writing about the brain is being done right here in our city, really a megalopolis of merged old-style cities taking up half the coast. Many of the best writers on the brain are here in our city, giving talks about their books and signing copies of them. Many of her brain books have been signed by their authors, whom she has met in person and asked informed, intelligent questions. She has noticed that during the question-and-answer period at the end of such talks the women in the audience don't ask as many questions as the men, or at least do not raise their hands with the same alacrity as the men. Therefore she makes a point of being among the first in the audience to ask a question, to lead the way for women and set an example. The idea that there are major differences between the male brain and the female brain is a canard, which is also a kind of bird—a duck rather than the false-cognate "canary," and to her mind among the more slow-witted of the bird family. She has no patience for ducks.

3.

The crow on the power line outside the window is gone. I am outside the window, looking in at her reading the latest brain-book in the oblong of sun on the futon. Outside it is neither warm nor cold. Inside she wears wool leg warmers and a halter-top with spaghetti straps, so the room's temperature is difficult to tell. The possibility of camouflage should never be discounted. On the outskirts of the city where there used to be trees there are now vast slums, shanty-towns with sewage in the ditches and foaming waste from the bio-tech labs. The shanties are built out of scraps, like bird-nests. The inhabitants of the shanty-towns piece together their shanties while the inhabitants in the universities and research centers piece together the sum of human knowledge. The most advanced brain science is being done with digital imaging. Together with the most advanced gene science and the most advanced theoretical physics the complete terrain of absolutely everything in the universe, the universe inside our brains as well as outside our brains, from the microscopic to the macroscopic, will be mapped, any day now will be mapped. It is already the dawn of the day when everything will mapped. But the word and indeed the very concept of "advanced" is retrograde, sentimental. One thing we are coming to understand is that human knowledge does not advance, in fact it does not move in a straight line at all. Knowledge does not advance but rather spreads, it does not march forth at the front of a column but spirals outwards, from a center. And not a single center but multiple centers, centers which move and shift depending on where they are viewed from, which puts the whole notion of "center" into play now, doesn't it.

4.

The Black Ops units are reading the latest brain books in order to conceptualize the most "advanced" techniques for surveillance and counter-insurgency. But the insurgents are keeping pace, unless it is rather the Black Ops counter-insurgents who are keeping pace with the insurgents, it is difficult to tell. The most "advanced" insurgents have web-cams in their bedrooms and perform acts of solo masturbation with some of the "advanced" non-lethal crowd-control weaponry that has been developed, just to show us perhaps that the secret we tried to hide by publishing detailed assembly instructions on the internet is out. There is a precise moment when the woman reading the brain books will put down the latest brain book and pick up a gun that resembles a paint-ball rifle, but which shoots pellets of a crowd-paralyzing foam. After which the men in the audience who raise their hands first had better watch out. Algorithms for telling how constraint-satisfaction works in neurally-plausible architectures might suggest a horizon for this event, but at another level certain sub-atomic particles with exotic names and even more exotic behaviors make narrower calculations a problem.

5.

But it is there nonetheless, this event, impending, it waits for us like a page in a book, even though the day has dawned when there will be no more books. It is the exact moment when the wire will be gone, just as there was an exact moment when the crow was gone and I had taken its place, a place that will also soon be gone. When the wire is gone I will be gone too, moving through the walls after the woman who has disappeared into her book or back into the shanty-town where another member of her cell fingers the remote. We are now able to conceptualize the most maze-like urban conflict zones in terms of a single plane.

Kate Hill Cantrill / *The Tree That Took Brooke's Faith Away*

It stood thick up from the bottom of the hill; from on top it looked no smaller, just lost within its grandeur. Brooke wrapped her fists around the rope some long-gone kid once tied around a branch. The twins, below—two boys well-known for mooning cheeks against their bedroom window, tossing underwear in the street for laughs—looked up at her and said: "Jump off the hill!"

She *would*, she said. The thing was, though, she couldn't shake the image of that dead dog she had found inside the black trash bag she thought could be first base, right before the twins said, Screw the game, let's swing. The thing was, though, she didn't know just when the dog had died, before—or god forbid—while within the twist-tied bag.

The twin boys laughed and waved their arms. Brooke saw they had a grown-up thing like interest spark inside their eyes. She knew her hair hung pale and wave-less. She knew she had a certain sort of swooping in her spine. She knew these boys, they saw these things. The dog, she thought, and when he died—they didn't understand.

But it was dead. This she knew. And here she stood, so head to head with this grand tree. *I should swing,* she thought. *I should run down the hill, clutch the rope, and swing like tether ball around the trunk.* The dog lay buried, now, where short-stops stood, and on its mound—the dirt now ruddy, upside-downed by her digging hands—she knew she placed one fist of stones she'd gathered by the old train tracks.

The boys cried: "Jump!"

The bag had been half-veiled in leaves. She thought it could be a fine first base. She thought at first it was filled with soil—it had that heavy feel of something from which trees and flowers sprung.

"Jump already! *Jump!*"

Brooke gripped the rope. *Who killed the dog?* The tree stood thick, went and up and up and up. The twins, they stared, way up, and up and up; and then Brooke feared—*where were the other baseball players? Where was the catcher? Where's the ump?*—she ran and parted ways with land. *Who killed the dog? Who tied the bag?* She soared and swung right down the hill, around the tree, toward the tree, toward the boys. She thought: He should have used his teeth. She thought: He should have fought and fought and fought. She thought: I think I know where next things go. I see it clearly from up here. And by the *here* she meant just where the pause occurred. Before descent, before the jealous world would grab at her right from the very pits of its so very needy core.

Jimmy Chen / *Let There Be*

There is an overpass above the highway. There is a barbed-wire fence that prevents pedestrians from jumping off the overpass. There are electrical wires above the overpass, conducting electricity from one side of the freeway to the other.

There is a bird that flies into a wire and falls onto the barbed-wire fence and dies. It stays there for days, dead. It rains, it pours. The sun, it shines. The bird is still there. The cars rush ahead below, driven by nervous people with unclear goals.

There is a large building on one side of the overpass. There is a two bedroom condominium inside. There is a man lying down on a futon after work, eating a tangerine and listening to this ceiling. There is an obese woman walking around loudly in her condominium. Her floor is the man's ceiling. There is no humor in this world.

There is saxophone in a studio. A man with excessively curly hair is playing the saxophone while being recorded. The notes that come out of the saxophone, and their relationships to each other, can be described by the word 'horrible.' He is famous. His music is horrible. His name is Kenny G.

There is a woman at work. There are two speakers. There is a CD drive. There is a play button. The woman at work has pushed the play button and Kenny G—or at least the digital semblance of his once manifest presence—plays horrible music. There is a stop button. It will not be pushed.

There is a man at work. He sits next to the woman who plays Kenny G all day. He is irritated because his job 'sucks,' a word used to describe an abstract yet distinctly relevant negative feeling one has about the existence of an object, including persons, and the object's relation to other objects.

There is a God. He creates light and sound. Everyone concentrates on the light and forgets about the sound, though there are sounds everywhere; the cars under the overpass, the obese footsteps above the ceiling, and the horrible music inside the speakers.

There is a man at work. There is a man at home. There is a man who can't sleep in his bed. There is a man who can't stay awake at work. There are dichotomies. There is the global economy. There is the falling American dollar. There is a mortgage. There is unemployment. There is welfare. There is homelessness. There is death. There is a man at work.

There is an overpass above the highway. There is a barbed-wire fence that prevents a man from jumping off the overpass on his way home from work. There is a dead bird hanging upside down from the barbed-wire fence. There is a man who stops to look at the bird. There is a sky happening behind all of this. It makes no sound.

Nolan Chessman / Bay of Smokes

I came to your town
and saw boulders
spilling off
the mtn.
bay of smokes
shied in loose
dress of sea
fog. Down
from the mtn.
your brother's coffin
in dirty shroud
of sea fog,
in rills
of debris
your brother's
coffin came
to be buried
in some ravaged
swimming pool.
Rills
of debris
sliding off the mtn.
In some ragged
swimming pool,
your brother
The Actor,
the clinking boulders
he heard, not
castanets strung
around his slight
neck, came
sliding off the mtn.

You said
he liked living
in the valley, your brother
The Actor
with twin cats
scarfed in varying
colors.
He liked living there,
his lifestyle
oversteepened in rock,
his cats scarfed
in colors,
gave them each
a sense
of self, he said,
oversteepened
from the storm,
had mined
a thunder
trail.
A gentle
sense of self, he said,
in the otherwise
faint dress
of sea fog.
Mined
from the storm
a thunder trail.
I came
to your town
and saw boulders,
a bay of smokes.

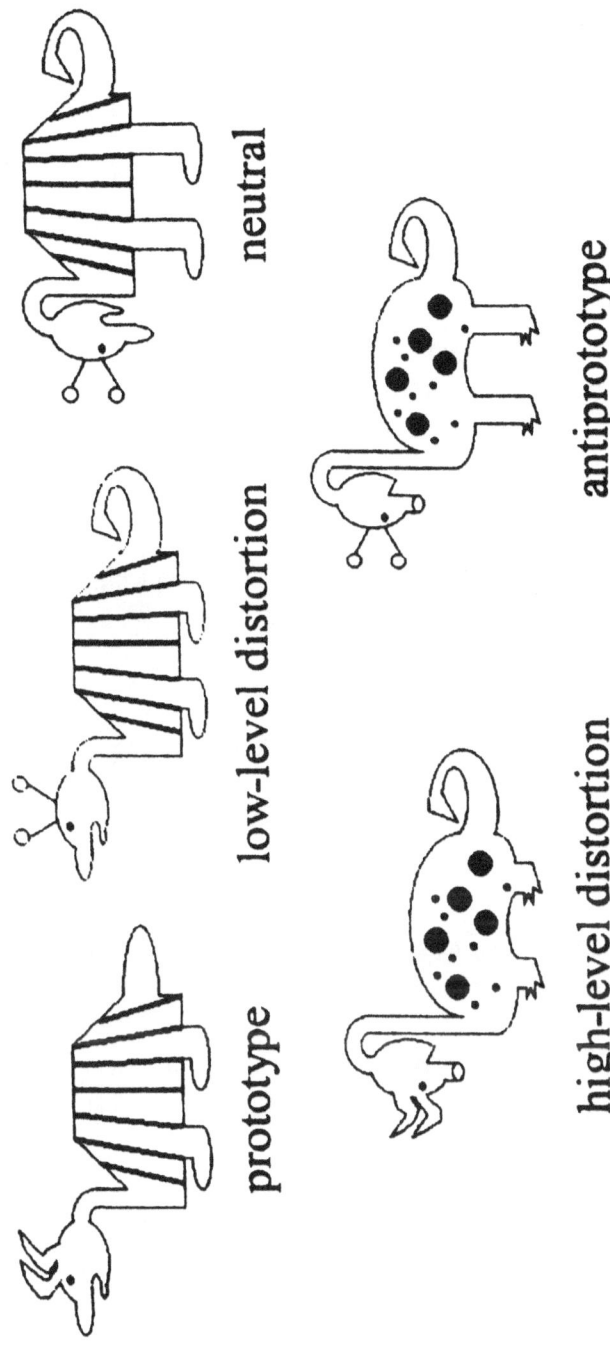

Figure 1. Examples of the stimuli used in Experiments 1 and 2. Prototypes contained nine prototypic features; low distortions contained seven or eight; neutral animals contained four or five; high distortions contained one or two; and the antiprototype contained no prototypic features.

Adam Clay / *In Light of Recent Developments*

We are not thinking of the president
    tonight. Even now, there is a maze carved in the corn

        not far from here.
The leaves pile up and we wait on the porch, sipping something,

        waiting for the leaves
    to self-combust and enter the air, the atmosphere, our lungs.

It's easy to mistake
    dust for smoke. It's easy to think of William Blake while the sun

burns a hole in our eyes. There is a certain labor I see in the sun,
    a type of hard work someone once

        warned me against, as if hard work and sweat
could wipe one from the face of the earth. Thinking of salted pork and a bridge

    fit for one car at a time. A detailed aftermath. An aftermath
    usually is. Memory like Blake seems to change.

When I think of nature, nature thinks back. Or nature blinks back. The man with a baby
    stroller filled with aluminum cans is now coming back up the street

    with a wheelbarrow. If that is what he had been saving for,
I wish I had often carried a bag of cans out to him. I once thought

    that expecting the worst was the best I could do.

Juliet Cook / *Self-Portrait as a Semi-Amorphous Entity*

Silly muffin-like thing
floating in a fizzy fissure.

Oddly fluffy little pink anomaly
sometimes has no ears, but still hears
through some manner of clandestine absorption.
A listening device a tiny warped sponge
implanted in the bottom of a silver foil
Baking and Party Cup w/ ruffled edges.
Impregnation by tainted sugar.

Inside a misshapen speech bubble,
toothsome words are birthed.
Incubate, overheat, burst. A spatter of
bloody latex, enamel, nougat, & nerves.

Through some style of self-referential abortion,
she evacuates doomish candy shapes. Inklings.

That's not a piñata she's beating
her own head against a doll house
door. A small demolition crew scuttles out
of a miniature bed; starts pulling her hair so hard,
her head flies off & lands in the cake pan.

That's not a piranha it's one of her
stanzas with gills glued on & heaving.

The spiky bite of a hellgrammite on its back
in heavy cream, swerving
like a possessed planchette.

The crescendo of sickly sweet stench
rising up from a pale blue fetal pig
it is time to dissect right now.

The Party Cheese Ball Mocks You

Glinting with tiny razor blades instead of almond slivers.

Squinting with burnt lima bean eyes from dust bunny heads.
Another cracked baking dish, another mushy brown apple
splat against the wall. Unpainted Still Life of Stagnant Mop
and Bent Broom Bristles, you think as you scrape your crummy casserole
down the garbage disposal. He's snoring, probably dreaming of someone
more gourmet and less frumpy. You wonder when

you turned into one of those interchangeable matrons
in a cleaning product commercial. Shapeless hair, dowdy underwear,
a plugged-in plastic air freshener discharging its automated spurts
of generic perfume. Maybe your scent is Stale Circus Peanuts
on a Bed of Wilted Bok Choy. Or Sweet & Sour
Apple Dumpling Gone Rotten, Gone Wormy.

The only reason you're not putrefying on a bland backdrop
of beige linoleum is because this batch of maggots was cooked to death
like a tired mound of pasty spaghetti with no sauce. Pallid leftovers.
From the top shelf, the party cheese ball mocks you. Perfectly-shaped
and about the size of a silicone implant, you think. Bedecked with those
tiny razor blades. It would spread so sweetly...

You want to melt it down, pour it on top the glutinous noodles.
You want to force feed it into the trash compactor, but that metallic clamor
might wake him and he doesn't see you that way. As a mutineer.
As a woman who could star in a commercial for tight jeans. He doesn't see
your eyes sting as you sweep away debris like soggy Lucky Charms
and dull elbow macaroni. When it is lodged deep in your throat,

he has no idea just how sharp a party cheese ball can be.

J. P. Dancing Bear / *Debris of an Automobile Giving Birth to a Blind Horse Biting a Telephone*

It's all fenders and hooves with you, she says: the raw light bulb in retrograde: the radiator taking root: rows upon rows of waiting for crops to grow themselves: you have a strong urge to buck: she's still wearing her *Miss Ingenuity* tiara: you can see how this is going: asphalt running its course to gravel and dirt: broken spokes: horseshoes: a need for stables and hay: rust jelly: this just makes your tires itch: *it's a crescent wrench and horse neck for you, Mister:* you're certain of the welding seams: land lines are ready: she's answering the phone: *yes, yes—he's here:* but your motor is revving

Figure 2. Targets of copying: Single daisy at four different orientations.

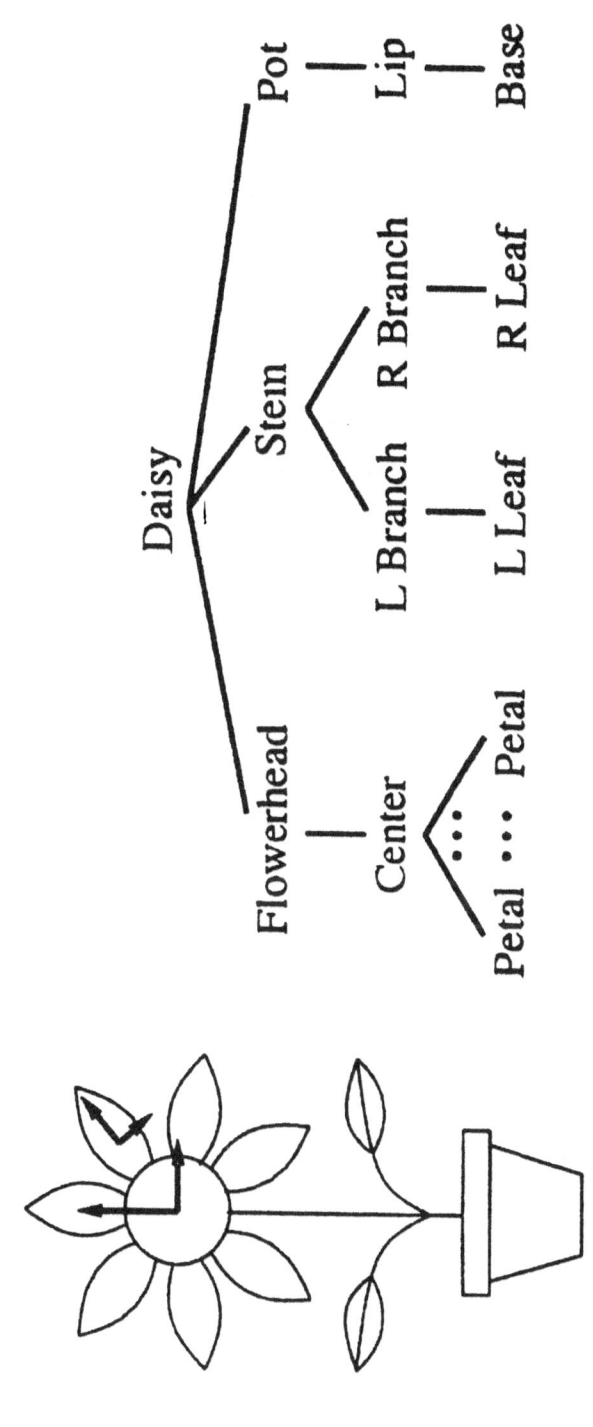

Figure 3. A daisy and its hierarchical representation, so that each part (*child*) of an object (*parent*) can be considered an object in its own right.

Lightsey Darst / *Land Use Planning*

Where they've irrigated, a green line.

Set, so that we would / speak the same tones
& phrases wherever we went, our imagined life

moving, generous or cruel, ahead like weeds along the world. Loosestrife:
purple, barely distinguished note among green. A cross is a place

for a bird to nest (here, in this Publix parking lot): to rest,
fold down an aching wing, remake the race. A girl whose bluebird eyes / question

of authorship? She might be ocean's, ebbing with the sweet cession
of low tide. While I, fastened to the bridge / and damp dream of it: crossing,

the brook's snake seen, winding away for hours, all night. Where, blessing,
they've planted an elm avenue, and where haven't they: they have the right.

Oh me, little seed, my crux. They will ask: what did you grow? Tightened
form inside a hull, unmirrored. Meanwhile what's ripe is splitting wide, though

for a moment brown and whole like this crow's eye.

President of evangelical university resigns
Retromancy. By looking over one's shoulder.

Kirk Lee Davis / *Night Picnic*

What is what, you ask?
So much is undefined.

    Astronomical is a word that rhymes with gastronomical.
    Language is often general in nature.

    Is is a weak verb. *What* is an interrogative all by itself.
    The trees are carved of wood. All their planks are tongue-in-groove.
    Ants are just as happy someplace else tonight.

    The moon is reflecting its better half.
    Stars are not the dead brought back as stars.

This is the spread we promised you.
This is eating out.
This devil's food is not half-bad.

    Dew is beginning to settle on the grass,
        but if it is okay with you, we suggest sta ing in the dark, even if it means
            we must ask *what is it*
                before and after every bite.
    The stars are something else.
        Which is to say, in the end, that we are what we've done,
            that this drink is strong,
and we are feeling it.

Jubilee at the Liberation of the Senses

Lookout Donkey—It's a shining corporeal supernova!
Mr. And Mrs. Political have got it together again!

Je suis en retard, Mr. Circumflex?
Let the poppy seeds eat their spongeycake!

The *Luftwaffe* is happy to see me!
Dance the whiteboy!

Okay now, everybody: barrel-roll those hips?
Simon says *pin the quail on the pattycake man!*

And helloooooo, Misti Applepants!
The Lord is willing and the flesh is Yahoo!

All free! All free!
What robot abdicator could forego?

Get up, Chipdog! Lock the backdoor!
The giant teeth! The torture wagons!

The fun is here to stay.

Report

As if in answer to the revelers' disbelief, a tiny note drafts up from the floor: *The months we spent in the dining room would prove to be the worst we would ever know. Our breaths flowered into coughs. The floor was dust, a trough we rolled into. A man would sit on a corpse's back just to tie his sweaty shoelaces. The ribcage of the corpse would collapse beneath him. Or it would not. Some people did laugh. Anyway there was no help to be given. Weakness is a thing with which every man, woman, and child must wrestle individually. Or so we had thought. In spite of his missing arm, one man managed to clothe himself in a fallen chandelier. The children to whom he gave bits of glass in which to gaze survive miraculously well.*

Report

For more than a year no one laughs, nor even speaks. That portion of our lives we spend out-of-doors would become the story of our lives. The children who lounge atop one another, waiting for us to weaken and break down with a story, grow disappointed. Some throw bits of shattered glass. Some rocks. Some tie shoelaces around our necks while we sleep at our stations.

Which of us survives does not matter. All of us to some degree, perhaps, as fixtures of the landscape. We grow roots—those who remain on long enough—where nothing else can. Each camouflages his memories: history will not single us out without our consent.

And so our sins stay sealed inside us as does blood in a body.

Nicole Cartwright Denison / *15 Conditions of the Tourist at Rest and in Motion*

(1.)

1. County Line, Road #23— Note the shoulders, haunch of the roadway, how workers delineate domain from destination, each listing with a natural inclination toward home.
2. The syncopation of traffic signals indicates relativity to motion in time, the distance between two points: westbound lanes travel into the future; eastbound, the past. The median watches patiently: everything must pass his way.
3. Intersections inform as to the culture of an area, a peculiarity of region, slice-of-life scenarios. Stripmalls indicate a predilection for conformity, the death of our former lives.

(2.)

4. A woman travels with a dog: breed unspecified. She tells you in line for breakfast that her sister is sick—this is all she will say, wanting to share in her stare, her automatically drawn mouth, you should know *what with*. Opelika lies at the end of 328 miles between them. You pass her barely making the speed limit at marker 41.
5. Compasses are ruined closer to the equator: magnetic, true North no longer registers. Spins are integral to discerning directions now.
6. Upon watching planes pass closely at the airport hotel you
    1. realize, after squashing an irrational fear of one crashing into this very window, amid the blinking lights and landing gear
    2. rationalize that Rate, Distance, & Time exist on paper only, mere measurements of experience, each a pleasure, however brief.

(3.)

7. Historical Markers abound: their tell-tale brown reminds how each acre became a battleground, blood memories kept vivid, a Confederacy hard won, lost again and again.
8. The journey of 1000+ miles continues with the rev of an engine, a fill-up, a tollway of potholes, as increments pass, clicked upon an atlas, this neverending blacktop abacus.
9. Last leg of the trip: highway hypnosis increases with each cloverleaf, every bridge iced in winter, stars adrift in cloudcover, their shadows shine our way, their light having dimmed long ago.

(4.)

10. Roadside Assistance: A highwayman possesses great nerve between guardrails and the whinny of engines. He extracts another wheel carved into pavement, imagines he hears the lingering screech, fingers skidmarks, reaches the dreaded end of the line.
11. One Lane Bridge: A headlight highbeams its way into infinity, at speeds which travel prismatic through December's icy dimensions; fog (or a swerving animal masquerading as such) its only enemy.
12. Another Roadside Attraction: Tourist Traps suffice for gag gifts, the scenes of a ViewMaster sometimes larger than roadkill, an invalid life, the curse of the homebound sure in its track.

(5.)

13. cardinal direction: another rootless origin: imaginary species: known for locations due Southeast in winter, Midwestern plains, shelves of books, state lines, national boundaries.
14. depicting the wind: a flower will wilt in tempest, best to conjure semaphore, translate this dialect of suffering.
15. compass rose: 32 points in the Portuguese; 16 modernized. if only it weren't whole continents dividing us.

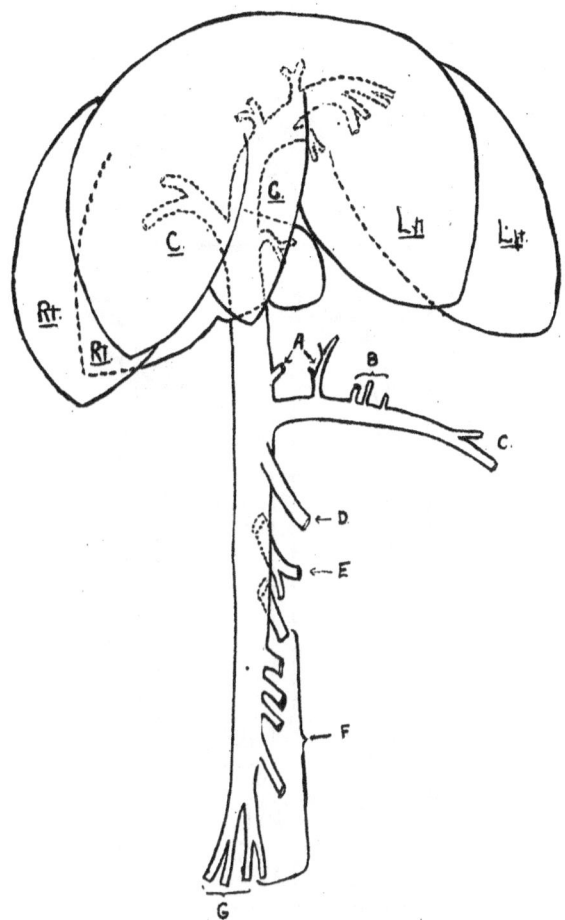

Fig. 1. Portal System of a Dog.

Showing the exact angle and side of entrance of each portal tributary. (*A* and *B*) veins from pancreas and stomach; (*C*) splenic vein; (*D*) small mesenteric vein; (*E*) duodenal and pancreatic veins; (*F*) jejunal vein; (*G*) vein from ileum and ascending colon.

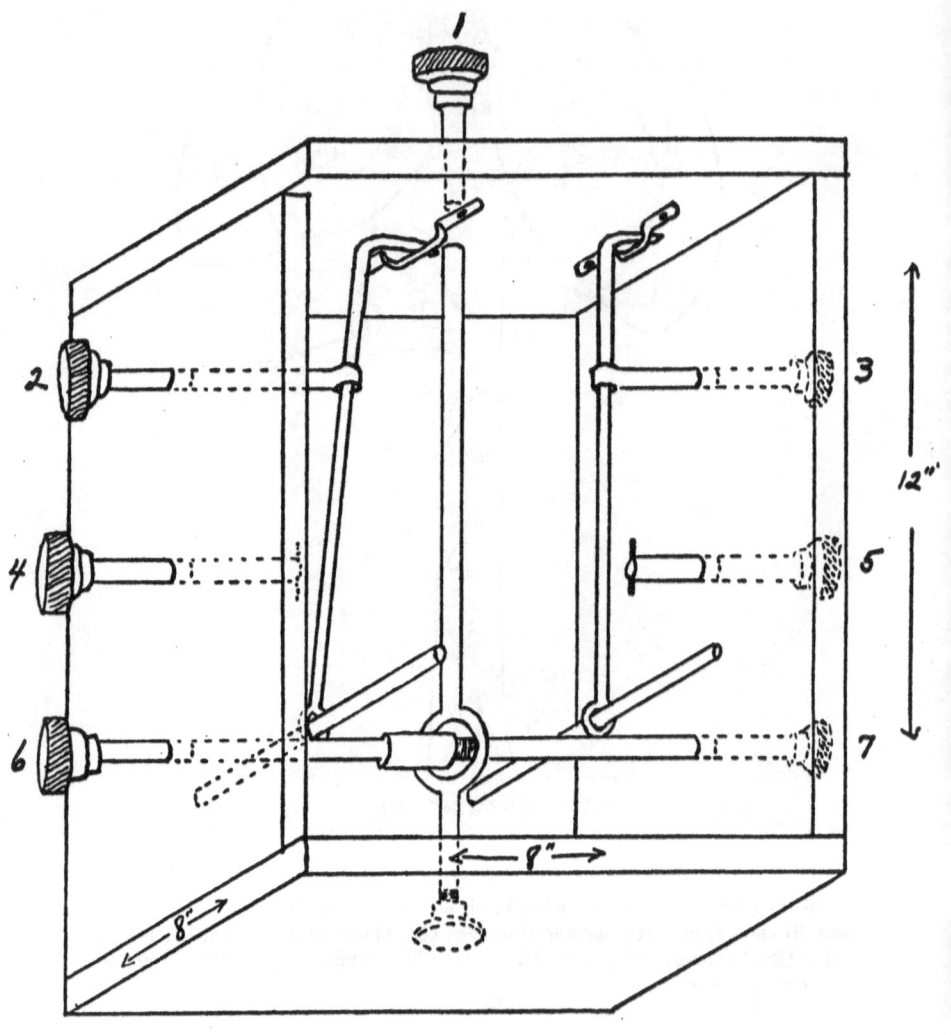

Fig. 1.   The problem box.

Adam Fell / *Bomb-Making Materials 1*

Christ their necks, their stunned necks,
lushed, hair up, the cheerleaders,
their throats, barest throats, collapsible
like wicks, lit, hands on mine, bare hands,
pulling my body up, up? yes, up, scared up,
from taserpoint & plasticuffs,
from boot-necked to the young bar floor,
the cheerleaders hold me, now, all, together,
above themselves, above the crowd,
above the riot cops, the shards of spit,
the brown glass spit, the gassing spit and eyes,
the choking kids, the townie kids
wrapping themselves in caution tape,
the college kids tipping over
the car they euphorically torched,
their groped mouths groping mouths,
their Mag-lite eyes bursting with happiness,
a happiness like a barricade,
but at least, god, a happiness,
a makeshift shield of happiness,
their chapped lips smudged red
on the chipped glass rims of harder mouths.
They full-finger the flames, they fist and clear
and fling their burning fists at me,
at me above them, high above them,
higher now, the cheerleaders raising me,
my bloodier threads, dripping already, already?
on the sidewalk, on the damp grass, on the parts
of the cheerleaders I will never be a part of,
the moving parts most stunning when they're still.

My Blood is a Family Automobile on Fire

My blood is a family automobile on fire but my toddling blood is un-
trained at being fuel so reverts to the purest form of accident, concedes its
blood-flush, fuel-heart, to the inferno, to the shoulder gravel, to the sky,
to the kids watching my blood crude to steel frame, roll cage, puddle to
primer, rubber, plastic, caustic smoke gauding sky, the sky quite above and
away from us, but right here so close to us, so close enough to clog the on-
lookers, the sheer-drags of their faces, our faces, lagging behind as brinks
of my blood crag and uncrag in the gravel. But shit,
now the kids are pulling out their favorite sources of water, someone's
brought the community school of alarms, it was only a matter of time,
but christ, where'd they get those powerful buckets? Suddenly so freshly-
trained, so taut with purpose, protocol, the inner Mag-lite glare of their
eyes? They're forming this human chain in the tampered lawn that leads
from the river to my blood, its melting treads careening into the gaunt
light sky, smoke-cake sky, my blood so curious, just curious, my blood, its
body so confused, shaken, it just wants to wait, so lets just wait and see if
I'll be smothered out by the weight of my own corrosive ash or if I'll burst
before you into a trick of collateral light for an instant.

Bomb-Making Materials 2

Downed, they let me, the cheerleaders,
the cheerleaders unhand me, all of me,
my fingers streak their beaded arms,
smudge their beaded calves,
their faces of powdered shell and sand,
turn away, they turn away
from me and seep and bank and settle,
they fade into doorways, into dorms,
to lofted beds, to futons,
the highest step in the stairwell,
anywhere recoverable,
anywhere no one can touch them.
They leave, and wet the city's morning
as they leave, and slur the lobes of me.
I am garbled, garbled but gallantly safe,
because of their kind bodies, their kind brains,
their footprints now just crushed grass, god,
my fuckt loyalty, my shivering, my snuffling brain,
my body, my body, the bar is gone,
the cheerleaders gone, I know they're gone,
but still, their blood-flush, pore-scrub,
I feel them through the cinderblocks,
the paint coats, I feel them on the one
soft cake of skin left beneath my arm,
the bruises of their fingertips yellowed
just to health, this health, thank god,
this health, thank god, for their kind brains,
their kind bodies, thank god, even alone,
even asleep, even in sweats, they broadcast,
on a loop, even as they dissipate,
unconfirmed reports of a new world
violently forming around me

with one less intimacy of glass
to have never put my fist through,
one less tongue to have never let in my mouth.

Matthew Gavin Frank / *After Piazza San Gallo a Firenze*

Painting by Ulvi Liegi (Luigi Levi)

We are not what we isolate
like the foot inside a street
the tongue inside a Starling

the brain, a salad overdressed
showing the first sign of rust
at the ribs, the opaque skeps

that to bees
are straw
cathedrals:

That one, behind us. Yours
isolating mine under
and under, the mouth

shuffling down beneath the sex
each snore, each smooth
straightaway, each spring

stands alone like new murder,
belly of hydrangea, belly
of all injustice,

the eye isolating itself
from its twin, and the throat
a backroad where sun isolates

its gravel. No: our love
is smeared senseless, right?
The accordion is dead, right,

some Venus and the ironed
dirge-light, the lemon flies
higher than its tree, once

in infancy, thirteen lift-offs
in my dream tonight, a healthy
shutting of the mouth

when a grandmother covers
her eyes with her hands
all morning, and promises

that all she's seen is still
and still alive.

Emily Kendal Frey / *Love Letter*

This letter is not liver-spotted or decaying. Ferns feather this letter. Never will this letter be referred to as an *institution*, nor will it *endure* or *persevere*.

This letter has lilt. Clearly, this letter lives somewhere lush. It does not possess charisma, only depth. This letter is not drenched in burgundy hues.

This is the one hundred percent tropical letter. Pineapples bruise and drip inside these words. This letter would not stop for a circus or a snack.

It is not boisterous or benevolent; however, it is breathtaking. Full bloom: unscented, oiled. Perhaps the tide comes in with this letter. The octopi

and the flaking salt, driftwood wearing seaweed necklaces, dribbling pebbles and shells. A rocky sunset in this letter. Illicit beach fires. Sunburned thighs.

All the limes split and squeezed, drying on the cutting board. A crow in the driveway. Indifferent aunts. One plane missed. Hungarian stew.

And then, he couldn't stop the feeling. He missed her pants and hips, lint between the computer keys, the purr of the electric toothbrush,

how she bent to pull tomatoes from the vine, dig at potatoes, her various hunchings. Nothing resigned. Their love expanded, like a balloon too

close to flame. He held the burning tip of it between his fingers. Scraped at the good root of things he knew. He'd buy her a sundress and grow

a mustache. Put a hand to her heaving clavicles, one cracked rib. The morning was a dewy one. She remembered standing in front of him in line, eyes reaching the same distance. She could smell the sleep on him. He, wondering at the arc between them, the dragonflies low over the water. Soon it would be their turn.

They wait, together, at the head of the line, each of them holding a particular weight, carrying something. They feel it move in their hands.

Matthew Glenwood / *John Henry's Tracks*

for T.K.

John Henry was a mighty man,
Born with a ten-pound hammer in his hand.
  —"John Henry" *

Some dirt-diggers in the Holy Land claimed to have found the bones of
Jesus and his family. Jesus' son, too. We'll probably never know for sure if
those were the holy bones or not. That kind of news could prove ungentle
to dreamers. Like finding the remains of Amelia Earhart under her front
porch steps, or the skeleton of a baby bird beneath its nest. We would
hope for a wider arc to the hero's journey than bones at the starting point.
It could be called bad news if Jesus, the alleged foreman of Heaven, left
bones behind. News that says *nobody's going very far.*

But it wouldn't be the whole truth. There is somewhere to go.

We can go sell our plasma for fifty American dollars a week.

The journey to the Biolife Plasma Center in Marquette, Michigan came
easy for me. I just had to follow an abandoned train track for a few blocks.
The track met the edge of the woods along the shore of Lake Superior;
rabbit, chipmunk and deer crisscrossed it as beasties would any ready
made trail, for there were no tracks left on that line. The rattle of my
mountain bike startled ducks from the shallow waters of the ditch along-
side. In winter, the flat, open space doubled as a cross country ski trail. You
might say everything ran on that track except for rails.

The region, too poor to have a reason to run its trains, pulled up many
of its train tracks, and commerce that way moved at the speed of wild
grass. The poverty of the Upper Peninsula of Michigan is probably why
the plasma company came to the Upper Peninsula of Michigan. That and
the local college students, the reliably poor. As any farmer with a bad back
could tell you, the easiest of tall crops to harvest is one that stoops to meet
the hand of the harvester.

At the plasma center, technicians tap into the natural resource of your veins. The process takes, at most, a couple hours, and you're paid for it. It's easy money, and couldn't come much easier; all you have to do is exist. The plasma company calls itself a "donation center", but really it is a selling center. Poor people coming to sell the one possession they unquestionably own: the materials of their being. Take away those materials and the world would have no more poor.

Our folk songs say that John Henry could drive steel harder and faster than any man. The job of a steel driver was to pound holes in rock by hammering a long metal drill held and rotated by another man known as a shaker. Dynamite was then dropped into those holes—tunnels blasted into mountain stone. Steel driving was done for the mean benefit of the train companies laying track across the nation. In other versions of the song, steel driving was intermixed with pounding spike into the rail lines.

One day a salesman brought a new steam-driven drill to the line. John Henry, fearing for his job and for the jobs of his fellow rail workers, challenged the machine to a contest. John Henry declared to his captain:

> Lord, a man aint nothin' but a man
> But before I let that steam-drill beat me down
> I'm gonna die with a hammer in my hand

John Henry won. But after beating the machine, he suffered a heart attack and died. That's to say, he could do no more work for the train company.

Like Jesus, no one can prove the John Henry of legend. Some stories say he was an ex-slave working for the Chesapeake and Ohio Railway during the Reconstruction days of the South, following the Civil War. People disagree on where, and if, the events of the song took place. One man thinks the contest of hammers happened in Talcott, West Virgina. But everybody knows that you've got to bite the coins that come out of Talcott.

About twenty years ago, a man in my hometown got caught in one of the big machines of the mining company. A rock crusher, if I remember right. He was the father of a classmate. I ought to have attended the funeral, but didn't. In those high school days I was discovering the books of the American Transcendentalists: Whitman, Emerson, Thoreau. "Transcendentalism" was a big word to me at the time. The idea of it is that you can ride your porch swing to the truth of all flowers. The notion sounds sound to me, still. But, being young, I felt as if I had inherited a mansion up in the blue air; as if everything wrong were, with an idea, suddenly right.

The daughter of the killed miner, my classmate, needed some consoling, but I was too shy, too awkward at social graces, to be one of the people to give it. I had no consoling to give. Her father was a good man of Finnish descent; he left behind a large family. The family had a new lesson to learn about the worst of all possible outcomes. As for me, I had my books which said spirit dances with matter.

Much of my life has passed since those books. Those Yankee writers of old are truer to me now than when I was young, and it's likely that I need them more now. But an idea isn't much true unless we are willing to wear its dirt. A frog of ugly sits at the center of true, and his appetite is Void.

Rather than the gift of a mansion in the sky, transcendence now seems to me a lifetime of lonely carpentry. Carpentry on a house nobody can see. And that house won't shelter from the rain, but make us wetter. Those who ply this trade might not finish even the front steps before the cold evening comes on, before the closing whistle blows. Maybe no one completes the house called Idealism— built, as it is, on the foundation that is the suffering of the world. The hammer is usually abandoned with much work left to do; it hums only a little while with the vibrations of the last nail driven, until stillness takes it.

Had the good miner's death happened today, I would've gone to the funeral. The fact about our portion of transcendence is that some of us get flattened in rock crushers. The fact is that there is blood on the machine.

And in the machine.

Sometimes the crashing waves of Lake Superior, powered by strong winds, sounded like a train through my apartment window. But, in the city of Marquette, the only real locomotion taking place was the centrifugal force of the Autoapheresis-C machine (made by the Baxter corporation) separating plasma from blood. The word "apheresis" is Greek for "take away".

In an introduction to the work song Take this Hammer, folk singer Leadbelly explains the shouts of hah! that pepper the verses, "Every time the men say 'hah!', the hammer falls."

> *Take this hammer*
> *Hah!*
> *And carry it to the captain*
> *Hah!*
> *Take this hammer*
> *Hah!*
> *And carry it to the captain*
> *Hah!*
> *You tell him I'm gone*
> *Hah!*
> *You tell him I'm gone*

Gone to donate plasma. This is how it works. You are made comfortable on a long, curved couch of smooth leather— a kind of psychiatrist's couch where nobody cares about your mind.

Hah!

At your side is the machine, the Autoapheresis-C. It looks harmless enough, a white box of plastic on wheels with dangling tubing. It is sanitary as a saint's glove.

Hah!

A friendly worker, clad in hospital scrubs, sterilizes your arm with a cool swab and slides a needle in your vein. You are connected to the Autoapheresis-C.

Hah!

First the collection phase. Your blood, sucked up a tube to a little spinning chamber of clear plastic, slips out of you with the speed of a snake on the run, staining the tube's transparency as it goes. Some of your inside is now outside.

Hah!

A chemical thinner is added to keep the blood from clotting. The spinning separates the plasma from your blood, as substances of differing densities are wont to do in a centrifuge.

Hah!

The plasma drips into the collection bag. The plasma is yellow, like foggy urine (for women taking the birth control pill, it's a pale green, like swamp water). You watch your plasma gather in the bag, a few drips at a time.

Hah!

Second, the return phase. Your red blood cells are returned to you through the same tube in which they were collected. Some of the outside is now your inside. Steps one and two are repeated.

Hah!

It's like that. Throughout the donation process, the Autoapheresis-C communicates by beeping. It tells the technicians when there are problems, such as low vein pressure. The donation center is riddled with these beeping sounds, like the metallic-bright chirping of birds on a machine planet. Once enough plasma been harvested, the machine beeps to signify the end of the donation process—the brassy, four-note heralding of a king—*da-da-da-DAH!*—a worker comes with a heat gun and cauterizes the collection bag severed and sealed.

The Autoapheresis-C then pumps a saline solution into your bloodstream to aid in rehydration.

When this is done, the needle is pulled from your arm. You are no longer connected to the Autoaphoresis-C. Consider yourself siphoned. Your donated bag of plasma is labeled, put on a tray with other bags, turned to ice in a freezer.

Once or twice a week, the plasma-ice cargo is loaded in volume onto a truck and delivered to medical companies. Businesses whose executives are themselves likely too wealthy to need to donate plasma.

Hah!

After donating, I returned home on the same train track I arrived by, a tight gauze wrap over the new hole in my arm, and new American dollars in my wallet.

If he asks you
Hah!
Was I running
Hah!
If he asks you
Hah!
Was I running
Hah!
You tell him I was flying
Hah!
You tell him I was flying!
—Leadbelly, "Take this Hammer"

A donor doesn't have much to do while the Autoapheresis-C frets at its machinations, but there is one task to perform. The donor is asked to pay attention to a strip of traffic lights on the side of the Autoapheresis-C; it tells how well the collection phase is going, how fast the blood is flowing.

Red means *not well.*

Yellow means *could be better.*

Green means *all is well.*

The donor is asked to make a fist and pump it if the colors fall from green to yellow or red. This increases blood flow.

It can't be a surprise, that in this society we are informed by lights when to stop and go.

According to a reporter on National Public Radio, long into the rebuilding of New Orleans after the devastation of Hurricane Katrina in 2005, even the simple act of driving a car was fraught with risk. Without working stoplights, four-way stops were a matter of guessing three other drivers' minds. But maybe this is true not just for a flood-ruined city. Maybe there are no traffic lights blinking anywhere with the kind certainty good citizens would like. Maybe the hesitance of a New Orleans driver at a four-way stop shows how it always is for the poor, who are asked to pledge allegiance to a gamble.

When surge water from Hurricane Katrina overloaded the levees of New Orleans, it took the lives of the excluded. People with nothing having it taken away. During those early crisis days, the nation with its flag flying on the moon couldn't deliver a bottle of water to a woman standing on her rooftop.

Where was government? The corpses of the poor spiraled down the flood streets, while those with the American dollars to pay for their escape told their survivor stories from neighboring states. The plumb-line division between the rich and poor—as divided as dry is from wet— tells what kind of country America has become, is becoming.

Two countries.

> John Henry's liddle mother
> Was all dressed in red,
> She jumped in bed, covered up her head,
> Said I didn't know my boy was dead,
> Said I didn't know my boy was dead.
> —"John Henry"

This is not to say that the poor are without means of providing for themselves. At the plasma center in Marquette, a donor is allowed to give plasma twice a week. The first time you donate, you get twenty American dollars. But if you come back within two days (it can't be the next day, the body needs time to generate more plasma), you get thirty. Maybe the poor can't "pull themselves up by their bootstraps", as the phrase goes—cheap bootstraps break— but they can bleed their boots for American money.

Corporate executives now earn four-hundred and fifty times what the average worker earns. Translated to plasma money: whereas the average plasma donor can earn up to $50 for two donations a week, a C.E.O. would be right to expect $22,500 for their two days at the plasma center, though their plasma drips the same.

I would as soon trust a corporate-driven democracy to care for the needs of its poor as I would trust in the pity of venom. Considering the fever of the profit motive in our nation, and seeing how slow the government was to react in New Orleans, the surest way to save that city would have been to contract-out the first responders—allow companies to charge poor people for their rescue. This would be done, no doubt, on credit—a kind of indentured servitude for being allowed to live. Profit-seeking sometimes moves with a speed kin enough to justice. But maybe it's not a government's task to come between the poor and their right to die unaided.

Government will be our rock is the promise of all the regulation we accept into our lives, but at the time it is needed most, government occasionally gets a headache and blurred vision, has to go lie down. It might need a few days to get itself together. Fail to pay your income tax and you will feel the full focus of government, in the shine of badge and the shine of gun, as if you were the most important person within its borders; begin to drown, on the streets of your hometown, and government reaches at you with ghost hands in the tardy dark, and you are one among too many.

This offends the idea of sound contract. Citizens are not allowed to fail their government, but they are allowed to be failed by it. That's a devil's deal. But poverty itself, best defined as a lack of options, is a devil's deal. John Henry, as an ex-slave, was free not to work on the railroad line if he chose not to, but he couldn't choose not to, because he was directed by the overseer of having no other choice. Call it freedom, if you like. That brand of freedom is spit on a handshake without the handshake.

Where is government? Not in stormy New Orleans. Over fifteen-hundred lives lost to the flood. Government may be somewhere, but not in stormy New Orleans. In stormy New Orleans, government was gone, gone, gone.

> *They took John Henry to the White House,*
> *And buried him in the san',*
> *And every locomotive come roarin' by,*
> *Says there lays that steel drivin' man,*
> *Says there lays that steel drivin' man.*
> —"John Henry"

I once scheduled a plasma donation too early in the morning. My heart rate was beneath the company's minimum requirement. I was feeling peaceful at the time; one of those unshakable good moods. The girl in charge of my screening said she would give me a chance to test again after I had a few minutes to wake up. This was encouraging news. While waiting, I walked to the restroom and did jumping jacks, push ups. I imagined chaotic, violent scenes, adventure scenarios requiring fight or flight responses. I made my mind a nightmare, and this worked swimmingly. My heart rate rose and I was allowed to donate that day.

I raised my heart rate on behalf of the machine, the Autoapheresis-C, but John Henry's heart rate rose against his machine, the steam-drill. I let a needle pierce me for American dollars, which required my reclining on a leather couch; he drove a kind of needle into rock for principle, which required his death by exhaustion.

I readily admit that I lost my contest with the Autoapheresis-C, because I never contested it.

For us moderns, the contest to keep up with the machines is a daily event. It could be said that technology has raised our heart rates by allowing us weaker hearts; we now do less work but we are less at rest. Machines have made us more immobile in our busyness. Sitting in one place has become our hard day's work, not because the labor is difficult, but because it is hard to give up the freedoms of the body, the joy of movement for which our muscles and skeletons were built. We walk faster than we used to, but not as far. We do many things at one time, we are more specialized, but we are barely defined; the lines that outline us flicker unclear.

In the early days of the steam-driven locomotive, trains moved at around twenty-five mile-per-hour. Slow enough to stop along their routes for fishermen, and berry pickers, and hunters, to exit into the wild and follow their hearts' pleasure into ambling afternoons. It made no matter where they got off the train, they could always hop back on when it made its return trip.

In our time—as bullet trains scream speeds of over three-hundred and fifty miles per hour—the train doesn't stop for ripe berries.

Are we better people for having a faster train? The sheen of technology tells us so. We are better people if moving faster is better. But the life choices within the minds of passengers throughout time always move at the same rate, that is, at the speed of timeless. A caveman, the first of gentlemen, might have moved slower (the pace of slouching is nothing to brag about, for sure) but if his choices were truer, he may have outpaced the astronauts. It might be that his integrity broke the sound barrier, even as his slogging feet begrudged the bog. That is to say, he traveled as far as a man could with the least technology. He walked so far he became us. And the easier we make our travel, the less we hear in his walking blues something of our own.

Now it's all new. The new trains are made to hover upon a magnetic field. At speed, they don't even touch the ground that they cross. If John Henry were to swing a metallic hammer on a magnetized track, he'd only swing it once.

Some say the year in which John Henry beat the steam-drill was 1872. There wouldn't be much point in John Henry challenging a drill to a contest now. Steam-drills have made way for industrial lasers. To compete in our day, John Henry would have to swing hammer faster than a ray of light could burn, which, currently, is approximately one hundred feet of rock an hour. Against such a machine there is no competing. Whereas it once took the strongest man around to fight against the machine, in our time only a man weak in his reasoning thinks it can be fought. This is progress.

> *The steam drill started at half past six,*
> *John Henry started the same time.*
> *John Henry struck bottom at half past eight,*
> *And the steam drill didn't bottom till nine,*
> *Oh, the steam drill didn't bottom till nine.*
> —"John Henry"

A mild controversy slipped into the media about an internet search engine's satellite images of New Orleans after Hurricane Katrina, or the lack thereof. The images continued to show a New Orleans before the devastation occurred. Some people alleged that not to show New Orleans in all its ruin was an attempt to hide the truth.

The satellite images of the category three hurricane as it crossed to the American coastline are stunning. With technology, we now have the power to watch an entire city drown.

What a satellite sees, I can't say, though many are the images which tell what it records. This star's-eye view is no doubt an upper-rung moment in our species' long ladder climb out of monkey. So very high, our machines. But there remains the question of what we do with the view.

Recently, an observatory was nearly destroyed in a California wildfire. We humans have a telescope that sees back into Time and shows us the fiery beginning of the Universe, but that great magnifier overshoots and overlooks the flames threatening—in present time— at its own observatory door, and so is lacking in the bi-focal. The weakest lens would have shown the encroaching fire clearer than one so very good. What is the Big Bang to me while my toes are roasting? As if simply to see is everything.

It means something, that John Henry named his hammer Lucy. His labor, his tools, were close enough to his heart to remain in his hand.

> John Henry's woman, Lucy—
> Dress she wore was blue;
> Eyes like stars an' teeth lak-a marble stone,
> An' John Henry named his hammah "Lucy", too,—
> Lawd,—Lawd—
> John Henry named his hammah "Lucy" too.
> —"John Henry"

I wonder if the makers of satellites name them "Lucy". It wouldn't mean much for me to name a satellite "Lucy", as my hands have never touched one. But a satellite knows me, if it wishes. I don't think I could see a satellite in orbit as well as it could show me my own face. If I happen to notice a satellite passing in the night sky, it might be technology, it might be a shooting star, it might be a messenger of the gods of old. No matter what that object in the sky is, it's the same as a train in the distance to me—one I am late in catching.

The tools we use today can go adrift in our hands. They don't always extend us, as a hammer does. They sometimes disappear from us.

Mississippi John Hurt said that John Henry could drive spike faster than any man because he swung two hammers, one for each hand. But John Henry's hammers are up there—high—spinning in near-zero gravity; the question is, who down here has the strength to grab them back?

> John Henry went to the tunnel
> And they put him in lead to drive,
> The rock was so tall and John Henry so small
> That he laid down his hammah and he cried,
> That he laid down his hammah and he cried.
> —"John Henry"

Sometimes during donation the Autoapheresis-C would make a peculiar beep, an alarm, and the machine came to a halt. A worker would come to my station, press a button, and reassure me that it was "just an air bubble" that had found its way into my extracted blood. The Autoapheresis-C would then destroy the bubble and return to its churn-work on my blood. If the machine didn't catch it—if an air bubble was put back into my bloodstream, and reached my heart—I could be donating all my plasma, in one sitting, to the undertaker. This "just an air bubble" popped up as much three times in a single visit. At such moments, my life depended upon the Autoapheresis-C not making an error.

Sure the risk was small. But so was my reason for being there. Had I died, it would have been for nothing.

Not for nothing, Biolife Plasma Services would have you believe. On their radio advertisement, the plasma company calls for heroes on a regular basis. *Help save a life today,* they say. And it's true. Without a doubt, donating plasma is for the greater good. It saves lives. Plasma can't be duplicated in a laboratory. When plasma is needed, nothing but plasma will do.

And yet Biolife is a business that requires the existence of poverty in order to turn a profit. It trades in the bodies of the poor to achieve its earnings. If you doubt this, ask yourself why there are no plasma donation centers located on gated streets with hilltop mansions.

In the defense of the buying and selling of vital body fluids, compensating donors would be unnecessary if enough people donated out of the kindness of their hearts. The fault, then, is not in the greed of the needle, but in the stinginess of the vein. Outright kindness, however, rarely marries well with profit.

It is true, without the incentive of American dollars, I would not have donated plasma nearly so often, maybe not at all. I made a lot of American dollars at the Biolife Plasma Center. What, you ask, did I use my plasma money for?

Rent, groceries.

Scar tissue is likely for long-term donors. One man donated his plasma so often he had a hole in his arm that wouldn't seal. You could say what the poor also sell is the integrity of their skin. I have a divot on my arm, from being pierced so often with the needle. The mark shows no sign of disappearing, even years after I stopped donating. I am branded.

Plasmapheresis may be mostly harmless, as the company would tell you, but the body isn't made to assembly-line-out its parts. To donate plasma is to temporarily weaken your immune system, so what the poor are also selling is a little bit of resistance to disease. For some donors, strains upon the body are more immediate. One woman collapsed in a local Wal-Mart soon after her visit to Biolife Plasma Services.

I saw a woman faint while donating. In the aisle across from me, a college girl, merry enough, in sneakers and sweatpants. Suddenly her eyes rolled, she blinked, she slumped over— way over—nearly fell off her seat. Technicians rushed to her aid. The on-duty nurse was called.

"Wake up, John Henry! John Henry, wake up!…John Henry, wake up!" they said in something just short of a shout, patting her cheek (though I doubt, in my poor memory, that her name was "John").

She woke up. She wasn't out very long. Groggily, she asked what happened, then vomited into the trashcan.

To those upper-middle-class moms and dads who gleefully sell their plasma, or the retired who gleefully sell their plasma, or college students who gleefully sell their plasma— who use the American dollars earned to meet car payments, or build a Christmas savings, or buy beer and a pizza—I have only these words: November doesn't rain on a fish.

To those whose life may have been saved by the plasma from out of my very own bloodstream, I'm glad for you, abstractly—but I didn't do it for you. *Well, what on Earth did you do it for, if not for me?* you ask.

Rent, groceries.

> *John Henry was on the mountain,*
> *The mountain was so high,*
> *He called to his pretty liddle wife,*
> *Said Ah kin almos' touch the sky,*
> *Said Ah kin almos' touch the sky.*
> —"John Henry"

WEALTH ENDED DEMOCRACY

That's what my sign said, as I joined the crowd of protestors outside the Superior Dome in 2004. We rallied against President George W. Bush making a rare stop at the Upper Peninsula on his re-election campaign. He slid into town on schedule like a goose on a slant of mud. He came to make his goddamn argument. I'm not sure what we were protesting, exactly—except him, his war, his policies, his rise to office, and probably his shoes.

We protestors were put in what was called a "free-speech zone"—a section cordoned off with police tape, as assigned by the very authorities we were demonstrating against. It wasn't really a free-speech zone, but a *go-stand-in-that-corner* zone. Local prison guards were on the scene to assist with crowd control.

Still, we weren't much removed. We stood face to face with the people waiting in line to see the President speak.

A man in the Presidential line saw my sign and scoffed. He looked robust, kempt, in his late twenties. His black hair was styled reasonably short, as my brown hair fell unreasonably long.

"*How* has wealth ended democracy?" he asked.

I had no fast answer. The words of my sign were three, easy to write in permanent marker (though they still came out crooked). My answer to him was a smile and a shrug. I had no real argument with him.

This was my first protest, after all. I only expected to stand. I didn't expect to be button-holed on my stance.

But he was right to ask. I should've been able to say what I felt, or I shouldn't have been there. This didn't make my sign untrue. But it made me a questionable holder of a sign.

Nearby in the crowd, a girl who seemed about ten years old was protesting, too. She was much more vocal than I was (meaning, she actually said something)—sometimes yelling slogans at the people standing in the Presidential queue. Her voice had gone hoarse with shouting.

Her parents, standing a step behind her, looked like professional protestors. They had what could be called that protestor-savvy. They were proud of their munchkin, it seemed, sometimes joining in, following her lead.

No blood for oil! she shouted.

No blood for oil! her parents shouted, too.

Interesting, I thought. Apparently protest can be inherited, like a grandmother's ring.

Other children were demonstrating, too. Children, opposed to the death of Iraqis and American soldiers overseas, though death, to a child, is likely no more real than the drawing of a derailed train.

The longer I listened to her hammering out phrases of outrage, the more it seemed to me that she should not have been there, either. At least, been there in that way. She was like me, voicing an opinion she probably could not explain, if pressed. Though not a fair comparison (she was short, and I was not)—there ought to be truth within the protestor to equal the cause.

John Henry was equal to his chosen cause. He was so equal, he matched it with his life. John Henry didn't win the contest of hammers because he was right. John Henry won the contest of hammers because he was true.

Someone might have asked the wee protestor, "What really matters to you in this world?"

And if her answer was honest, it might be, "I don't know yet."

Maybe, given the time to think, free from the bias of her parents, the girl might have chosen to stand in line to see the President. Her freedom to do so would be worthy of defense.

I left the protest that day less sure of the free-speech ground I had been assigned to stand on. This is not to say that one should have to be per-fected before fighting injustice. But, when the battle comes, if one is only half-present, it is little different than not being there.

This extends. Sources tell me that it is bad to not care about the down-trodden.

Downtrodden. Say that word and prisoners bake you a custard. Heaven's rickety gates creeeaaaak open with all the glamour of a Vaudeville backstage shooting, when you say that word. Downtrodden, downtrodden. There's noth-ing that shouldn't be done for the downtrodden. Gather all the buttercups in the world in one be-glimmer-dazzled petal pile, and leave a note atop it that says *These are for the downtrodden*. An astronaut launching from Earth, on the verge of achieving escape velocity atop a towering cone of fire and smoke should— stop— mid-air—and come back to the ground and…care for the downtrodden. It means nothing to be *up*trodden. Forget it. Uptrodden will get you no favors around here. If you find yourself uptrodden, then you'd better have wet tears in your eyes for the downtrodden, or you are lower than you might be, and not nearly low enough.

Why should we care for the poor? Because the poor, like baby birds, *cheep cheep* loudly for the good worms? *You are cheap, cheap for not giving us some!* Poverty has always carried a begging bowl, and there ap-pears to be no natural law that says the rich should fill it. In Nature, baby birds that fall out of the nest are often left to die. And sometimes their stronger siblings block them from food, to the point of starvation.

If I choose to let you die from want, brother, sister, I wonder who would stop me? The cattle-whip of platitudes that tells me wealth is wrong, and makes me shrug and shrink when it's snapped overhead by anyone who happens to pick it up? Snap it at me, if you wish. Even a mean law to make me feed you would not stop my mean heart, which rolls all over the downtrodden like a flaming boulder, and treads them down more.

Now the straw boss came to John Henry
He cried, "This tunnel is caving in!"
John Henry just laughed at the straw boss and said,
"That's nothing but my hammer sucking wind,
Lawd, Lawdy,
That ain't nothing but my hammer sucking wind."
—"John Henry"

If I were a John Henry, I wouldn't have let that Autoapheresis-C machine suck me up. I wouldn't have sold my plasma for American dollars. Maybe, on a good day, I would've given it to my brothers and sisters for free. If I were a John Henry, I would've driven steel against the Autoapheresis-C, and spat at the American-dollars-idea to push selling my body as an option in my poverty.

But I'm not a John Henry. That work continues. I'm trying to lay enough track within myself to make an uninterrupted line possible between the two coasts of my loves and hates, but there's no telling how far that steel will reach, what mountains block the crossing. Maybe there isn't as much time to finish as I had hoped. Maybe, for delays, that track will never be complete.

As he was dying, John Henry said:
"Captain, I've hammered my insides in two,
Lord, I've hammered my insides in two."

We sing John Henry's song, and keep singing it, because he was a hero. John Henry died defending an idea in his brothers' and sisters' name. And what of that? I imagine the crowd that watched John Henry drive steel that day, watched him win over that machine, watched him lay his hammer down and collapse in the dust—I imagine they hung their heads in sorrow, for a time—a good, long time...and then went to the bar for a cold beer. The steam-drill he conquered was likely ready for work the next day, if not the next moment. The company still had track to put down. And the poor returned to the routine of their poor lives. In versions of the song,

John Henry's lover Polly Ann picks up his hammer after he falls, and she then drives steel like a man— but we are left to infer why. Though my heart would like to believe she swung that hammer for love of her fallen man, love is a track where every train runs on time, and I can't make such a schedule. It might be safer to say that she did it because she needed groceries. Heroes of tomorrow, take note: if you make your heart explode for invisible principles, the results may be invisible.

So was that railroad track worth John Henry's dying? In the song, John Henry knew full well, even as a child, that "this hammer'll be the death of me." To him, fighting the machine was a battle worth all his effort, and all his effort meant his dying. Maybe what is needed in our society now is to stand like John Henry did. That's a heavy hammer to swing; heavier than fourteen pounds, for sure. Still, my hands tell me that a good idea is a hammer worth swinging. And any hammer worth swinging is the only one worth swinging, even if we are driving invisible spike.

I don't believe that John Henry died so the trains could run. Why hammer a golden spike into a railroad track that carries mainly coal? The fretting weighs more than the freight. It was probably more important to him that a human built the track than a train could chug the length of the continent. The aim of his labor was purer, prouder than steam power; more deeply driven. I think John Henry, born a steel driving man, was laying a different track entirely; an invisible one.

> White man saw John Henry's
> Steel a-goin' down;
> White Man says,—"That man's a mighty man,
> But he'll weaken when th' hardes' rock is foun',—
> Lawd,—Lawd,—
> He'll weaken when th'hardes' rock is foun.'"
> —"John Henry"

What if we lived in a world where religion, philosophy, government, technology, social justice, were not enough to get us through? As false as they were true? Not support, in their last, tested strains, but shackle?

When our beliefs fail us, what would we have for a foundation upon which to stand and say *here!*—say, like John Henry, *here and no more!* What if there was no John Henry, never was and never could be—what would be left?

Our plasma.

> *This is the hammer that killed John Henry*
> *But it won't kill me, no, it won't kill me.*
> —Mississippi John Hurt, "Spike Driver Blues"

—

* Most of the John Henry lyrics were taken from this marvelous website source, and apparently gathered by a man named Guy Johnson: <http://www.ibiblio.org/john_henry/lyrics1.html>

antics with semantics

Brent Goodman / *Science Fiction*

For this role I learned to play the Theremin. The plot unfolds: after the
spaceship tears through the water tower all the cows' milk turns to ash.
At first, we welcome them in the cool shaded corn rows. Then green army
men descend in their own shiny aircraft. Before our pets go missing, before
our children turn against us, the general radios the president. I play the
scientist who insists they're more like us than anyone might imagine.

Loren Goodman / *Pinsky & Me*

Pinsky is concerned
with the medium
   of poetry
& I with the extra large

Idris Goodwin / *Desperado*

amongst handiwork she is a lightning bug
bolting, yo-yo, alive

only stare, envy washed, and
she is without inner monologue

or weight. she floats then
dips, a golden seesaw

within patterns, perfect pitch
where I find myself. terrified

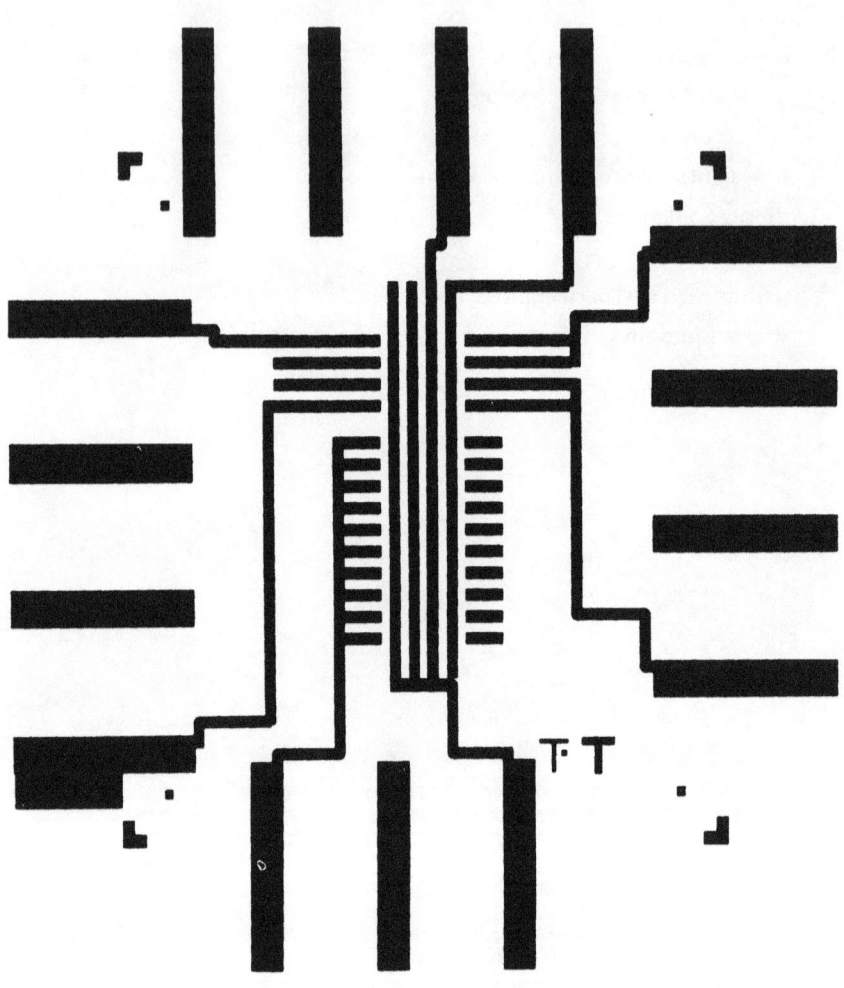

Fig. 9—Reticle produced by the electron beam.

Amelia Gray / *There Will Be Sense*

And then, though they had a choice, the doctors put a generator in my heart, and they gave me a magnetic band to wear on my wrist which I must pass over my heart when the old feelings begin again. *Arnold*, they say, *you are certainly a special man.* The following is true:

1. Because of a history of powerful migraines accompanied by the trilling melody of seizure, I have certain precautions installed by man in my body preventing me from biting off my tongue
2. A side effect of the migraines is a disorder called Alice in Wonderland which causes worlds to complicate outside of my control
3. The word "special" often carries both positive and negative connotation

Jeannie serves me tostadas at the café, the gold cross on her necklace (warm, no doubt, from her skin and the heat of the deep fryer) dangling close to my sweet iced tea. It's the first thing I see as I come out of the dangerous haze, and I feel small and close enough to the cross to make a leap for it. I'd like to dig my fingernails into the soft cooling gold and balance on the arm of it as on a tree branch, holding the chain for support.

"Watch the plate," Jeannie calls from miles above. She throws herself back like a gymnast and vertigo pins me to the wall. The generator in my heart ticks one sad farewell tick and silences. I miss it already.

"I almost had a seizure," I say.

"I sneak up," she says. She points to her soft-soled shoes. "Sorry if I scared you."

"You didn't," I say. "It was in my head."

Jeannie smiles like an acolyte. "Tostadas are the special today," she says.

"They look special."

"Are you Catholic?" she asks, folding the plate's towel under her arm. There's nobody else in the restaurant except the cook who, finished with the obligation of soaking a corn tortilla in tomato puree and calling it a tostada, is lighting his cigarette on the grill. "I thought I saw you blessing yourself a minute ago," Jeannie says. "I'm just wondering."

"God is very important to me," I say, though what she saw as spiritual devotion was an act that has always been purely physical, my body prompting the machine to prompt my heart to regulate my brain's foolish attempt to revolt against the whole. Religious women are often interested in me because they misinterpret the event. I am often interested in them because they remind me of my mother. This is not strange.

Jeannie rolls silverware and talks to the cook. My tostada depresses me and when I leave, I feel it in my stomach as a whole. My stomach conforms to the shape of the corn discus. I avoid eye contact out of shame.

This town has one fountain, and I pass by it on the walk home. People come to watch the water go up and down, and they throw coins in the fountain and feed the birds around it. It's an idyllic little scene. What the world needs is more fountains. The corn disk is cutting the soft lining of my stomach in half and I lie down on a bench, feeling embarrassed and oppressively blocked. The only other person at the fountain today is a woman wearing a zippered pouch around her waist. She sits with her feet in the water, looking in, and every few minutes she reaches, takes a handful of money, shakes her hand a few times (water's qualities in sunlight: mirrors, jewels, fire) and drops it into the zippered pouch.

"That's illegal," I say.

"I reject law," she says. "This fountain has no laws."

"What about gravity?"

"That's just a good idea."

The tostada grows three times larger in my stomach. I have the brief sensation of the woman shooting far away, into the trees at the edge of the park, me tied to the bench without hope of pursuit. The feeling passes before I think to move my arm.

"That money goes to charity," I say.

"What do I look like?" the woman says.

I tilt my head to look up at her. She's wearing blue linen pants, wet at the calves from the fountain, and a white shirt. Her hair is tied up with a yellow kerchief, which has the effect of pulling her features up and back, lengthening her neck, brightening her face. I feel heat like a rash. "The

Virgin Mary," I say.

"The Virgin Mary?" she says. "That's strange."

"No, it's not."

She stands up. Her zippered pouch drips water down her leg. She is unusually tall.

I have to shut my eyes. "I'm sorry," I say. "I'm disoriented."

"Story of my life," she says. When I open my eyes, she's vaulting over a line of bushes on the other side of the park. I think, good. The world needs tougher religious artifacts. Everything you find on Sunday morning is too delicate. Candles burning over white linen. Transferring the wine from vessel to vessel, chasuble sleeves hanging perilously close. You can buy all this stuff from a catalog, but it's expensive. Sometimes, it comes blessed.

The fountain is very close to my home and at my home's heart is my medicine cabinet. Something feels very strange about the container of my body. As I was getting up, the corn disk hardened into a circular saw blade and went to work on the flesh of my organs. It consumes and spins faster and threatens my spinal cord. My brain howls in protest. I want darkness and my bed and the calming mechanism of a great deal of medication.

My brain says, careful what you wish for!

The next day, Jeannie serves me King Ranch chicken (the finest chicken dish named after a bastard since General Tso's) at the café. She has her hair pulled back.

"Your hair looks nice like that," I say.

"I wear it like this every day," she says. This sounds a little accusatory and I feel like apologizing for not noticing and then I resent the desire to apologize for not noticing because it's not as if noticing her is my responsibility. I have lately been thinking about responsibility. The chicken is congealed to my plate under a solid grease-mound of cheese.

"What are your responsibilities?" I ask Jeannie.

She glances at her other table, two women who are also having the King Ranch chicken. It is the special. "I take orders," she says, looking back. "And I bring out water and I serve plates and sometimes I say 'that plate is hot' and I roll silverware, and I cut lemons and limes and I clean the women's restroom and I wash the windows and I change the specials board and write receipts and make change."

"That sounds like a great deal of responsibility," I say, thinking of lists (1. bring out water 2. serve plates 2a. that plate is hot 2b. I hope you enjoy the food 3. roll silverware 3a. this silverware is heavy and right 3b. what am I going to do about my problems 4. cut 4a. lemons 4b. limes 5. clean 5a. windows 5b. restroom 5c. specials board), "but I meant in your whole life."

"That's a lot more," she says, smiling.

"I imagine so."

She picks up my menu. "What are your responsibilities?"

"To keep my body alive, and my mind well."

"That's it?" she says. "Well, you're lucky."

I cut through cold cheese with the side of my fork. "I am the luckiest man alive," I say. "I am the luckiest man in the history of the free world."

"Don't you have a job, though? Don't you have any goals?"

These questions make me uncomfortable. There is a poster behind her of peppers from around the world and I wonder, which pepper would be the worst on the tongue. Then, if you swallowed them, which pepper would be the worst in the gut, and how would the burn differ. Jeannie would not be interested in me if I told her that I got checks from my mother and from the government and, though I respect the necessary existence of each, that I dislike both as sources of revenue, and that my goal is her, or someone like her. These are normal ways to think but no way to talk to a religious woman.

"My goals are to be alive and well," I say, "and to be closer to God."

"Those are good goals."

"I want to get so close to God that God has to file a restraining order."

*

QUESTIONS FROM THE FLOOR

Q: Why does Jeannie like you?
A: Jeannie appreciates my honesty and understands that there is not

nearly enough of it in men in the world these days. She has not given it much thought.

Q: Is it possible that she will break your heart?
A: She would need a much larger magnet.

Q: Do you expect us to believe you?
A: You have absolutely no choice.

Q: We resent this, Arnold. Please give us a reason to trust you.
A: Gladly: You have absolutely no choice.

Q: Don't you feel that God is *so beyond* caring what is going on down here?
A:

*

The fountain is broken. The water in the concrete basin is still, and the pumps are shut off. A man in work clothes is bent over an electrical box I never noticed, twisting wires. I think of the electrical box in my chest and feel a little sorry for myself.

"The water is powered by electricity," I say to the man. "Doesn't that seem like a cop-out?"

The man pulls a crimping tool out of his box. "I'd be out of a job if it wasn't," he says.

"What are your responsibilities?"

"To keep food on the table," he says, turning his attention to the electrical box.

"You're lucky you don't live on a boat."

"What's that?"

"You're lucky you don't live on a boat on the ocean. It would make things difficult."

"Fishermen make a lot of money these days," the man says. "I was watching a show about it. It's profitable but dangerous."

We live in a world where fishing is sexy. "My responsibilities are to keep my body alive, and my mind well," I call out to the man working in the electrical box.

"That's hard to do on your own," the man says. He's hiding in his work clothes. All I see is blue denim and brown belt. This man is a novice practitioner of the electrical box and is growing smaller by the second. This is terrifying to me and I call out, "I'm doing the best I can!"

I'm very worried that the man will become the electrical box and that the fountain will never be repaired. "Please be careful!" I yell desperately towards the smooth denim, a hanging curtain now, over the electrical box. My hand comes up, my wrist, and I start the generator in my chest. The battery is tiny and creates a small alien warmth as I am brought back hard to the world.

From my brain, an urgent message:

Why did you do that? We were all about to have a good time. If it weren't for you and your precious medical science, we'd be orbiting Saturn right now and watching the stars fall. You call this keeping your mind well? We're all well on our way to crushing boredom, that's all. But don't worry about us. It's not as if we power your dirty shell through this world. It's not as if we spend all day waiting for a nap in the sun, only to find you jogging us back to your own pointless day-to-day. We have nothing better to do. Please, continue.

My brain is diseased with logic.

Jeannie tells me that the daily specials in the café are always the food they didn't sell enough of from the day before. She points at my sloppy joe.

"Taco meat from Thursday and marinara sauce. Some ketchup."

"What about the King Ranch?"

"Chicken quesadillas. The tortillas went stale."

"How late do you work tonight?"

She looks at me and doesn't say anything. Under the table, I rip my napkin in half, and then in half again, and again and it's snowing white paper over my shoes.

"You might want to come to my home for dinner," I say.

When Jeannie and I walk to my home, the following does not happen:

1. We turn miniscule but not unimportant, and find that blades of grass have their own weapons, though they are weapons against small insects, who look like demons at close proximity
2. The sidewalk turns liquid and claims us, drawing us deep through hot sharp earth, where we meet those from generations past as well as some people working in a coal mine
3. A wise man confronts us and suggests that the *Pieta* is the most beautiful piece of art ever made by a human in the history of the world and while I don't disagree I think it might be even better as a fountain

I do, however, realize that Jeannie is essential to not one but both of my responsibilities and is therefore very precious to me. She nourishes my body with her daily leftover specials and she is strong and essential to the health and safety of my mind. It is when I look dreamily at the pendular motion of her golden cross that I realize I feel entirely well. Inside my heart, the generator rides the thumping aortic valve in blissful, silent contentment. Jeannie's hair flows behind her like a river. I am in ecstasy.

In my home, Jeannie looks around. "It's cleaner than I thought," she says.

I offer her a mint because I'm not sure what else to do with her. We are both very shy, and not used to interpersonal communication outside the arena of the café. I do feel very shy. My generator feels that I feel very shy.

She pinches a mint with clean fingers. We both smell like ground beef.

"Where did you get this box?" she says.

"From a catalog."

"It's adorable," she says, taking it and turning it over in her hands. "Isn't this what priests keep communion wafers in?"

"A pyx," I say. "It came blessed."

She looks around the room. Her eyes see: table, books, parament, pyx collection, stove, palm fronds, window, stained glass. In the stained glass, she sees tiny bubbles which contain worlds.

"Did all this come from a catalog?" she says.

"The oven came with the apartment."

She laughs, and then she stops laughing. She looks at the oven and I want to tell her that it actually did come with the apartment and that's not a joke and she's really quite kind to come over for dinner and I'm sorry that I didn't make anything and moreover that I don't have anything in the house to eat because I usually take my meals out because it's good for the spirit and as usual what's good for the spirit is bad for the wallet.

Jeannie sits down at the table and begins to cry. I touch her hair with my lips and her head is warm and smells like a glass of milk. She sobs and holds her fists closed on her knees.

"I'm sorry," she says. "I'm frightened."
My fingertips brush against the place where her hair is drawn up in a ponytail and I say, "you certainly shouldn't be frightened of me, if that is what you are frightened of."

"No," she says. "I am having a fight with my husband and I have nobody to talk about it with. I am frightened he will leave me," she says.

*

(Then, a terrible thing happens: My brain leaves the picture entirely. The room goes completely black, and the spotlight comes up on the two of us—Jeannie at the table, with my brainless body propped up behind her. Someone coughs. The curtain man lights his cigarette and digs into the fuse box.)

JEANNIE (in tears): I am frightened he will leave me.

ARNOLD: Don't be frightened. Please, let's talk about it, between the two of us. Let's work out a solution for you.

JEANNIE: I can't do that. I feel awful about doing this to you, burdening you with this.

ARNOLD (putting his hands on her shoulders): It's no trouble at all, my dear. Can't you see? I care very much for you. How long have you been married?

JEANNIE: Six months. He's a good man, he has a good job. He's great in bed—

ARNOLD: And why don't you wear a ring?

JEANNIE: We're getting rings tattooed on our fingers as soon as we can find the perfect artist. I figure it's more lasting that way.

ARNOLD: So what's the problem?

JEANNIE: If you'd let me get to it—

ARNOLD (*laughs suddenly*): I just don't see the problem then, pretty girl like you, a newlywed, striking out in the world with a sensitive and handsome man—

JEANNIE: Whoever said he was handsome?

ARNOLD: Your responsibility overall is to care for your own life and your own handsome husband because he is a lucky man and to see you sad should be one of the great sadnesses in his life and I'll tell you that honestly, it should be one of his greatest sadnesses.

JEANNIE: Whoever said he was handsome?

BLACKOUT.

*

"What gives?"

"Sorry." I reach for the wall, feeling for the switch. When I find it, she's looking at me with fish eyes.

"I think I'd better go," she says. She stands up and I shrink back in my chair. "But thank you for the advice."

She is a tower of a woman! In the center of my seat, I am acutely aware of the false-feeling velvet under my hands.

"Would you like a glass of water?" I ask the tower of Jeannie.

"No, thank you." She reaches across the room and puts her hand the doorknob. She fills my apartment and I cower in the low cover of the chair cushion. And then the *whump whump* of my brain as it comes down the stairs two at a time, looking for breakfast. As she leaves, she sees a man alone at his kitchen table, blessing himself before the invisible feast.

After that, as after all great tragedies, the days go by:

Jeannie serves me meatloaf at the café.

Jeannie serves me spaghetti and meatballs at the café.

Jeannie serves me pork barbecue and french fries at the café.

Jeannie serves me breakfast tacos at the café.

Jeannie serves me fajitas at the café.

Jeannie serves me onion soup at the café.

Jeannie serves me quesadillas at the café.

Jeannie serves me chicken fried steak at the café.

Jeannie serves me grilled cheese sandwiches at the café.

Jeannie serves me steak and eggs at the café.

Jeannie serves me baked potato at the café.

Jeannie serves me tomato soup at the café.

Jeannie serves me pork chops at the café.

Jeannie serves me cheese crisp at the café.

Jeannie serves me ham and cheese at the café.

Jeannie serves me fish sandwiches at the café.

Jeannie serves me chicken salad at the café.

Jeannie serves me corn dogs at the café.

Jeannie serves me tamale pie at the café.

Jeannie serves me vegetable soup at the café.

Jeannie serves me macaroni at the café.

Jeannie serves me chili at the café.

And one day, I come home to find Virgin Mary sitting at my kitchen table.

"Hey there," she says. She is eating mints from my favorite pyx.

"How did you get in here?"

"I try doors. Aren't you that guy from the fountain?" She offers me a mint.

My hands are huge and I am concerned they will flatten her in the course of my reach. She watches my awkward progress with careful pin-hole eyes. When I touch the pyx, she snaps it closed.

"What is life?" she asks.

"Alive," I say, "and well."

She nods once, grandly. "I thought you might know, if anybody did."

4. At the appointment time, the doctor opens the door and invites the patient into the consultation room, through the small vestibule. The low ceiling of this space intensifies the feeling of intimacy.

7. As the patient leaves the elevator at the main lobby, before opening the door to the sidewalk he gets a glimpse of the outside through the glass panels flanking the door, converse to his view when entering, completing the cycle.

Marj Hahne / H — Hydrogen 1

Had the Blüthner piano not been removed from the Hindenburg to save weight (though it was aluminum custom-made, though hydrogen's a less dense lift-gas than helium), what brief dirge would've mourned the thirty-seven-second burn in its downward blazing? How many leapers, in that half-minute of hammers striking strings, would've stopped short of their vertical drop, followed the float of notes upward to see a fire lighter than air?

No one knows the what-if future; no theory can light the combustible past: sabotage? static spark? puncture? The most abundant element in the universe is flammable, love. Above us I looked before my leaping, you a shadowy ground. Shifting? Last night you let me play "zen" in Scrabble, though the word's a proper noun. Though I didn't let you play "lite."

John Harper / *You of Clown #2*

Things to do today in the seminar making me up,
painting my next move
up in soda-fashion,
in this dreamt of canvas
of so-so merry weather—

saunter yonder—ok;
get a handle—ok;
quit the solemn varnish & context—ok;
know now is the sole time of all

by vanishing into hazy loud silence, no letters thence—I want this,
I want that—
not a single, good-tasting, lasting drop of an answer
under my circus-wear,
where behind feels the wheels of fear, and ahead

is large, open wind—ok.

I haven't done anything—ok.
Anything I'm not usually ashamed of: the address
is as last time, as almost always the case, and the time

before, etc. What is it—real life
        and then fake life?

Luis Felipe Hernandez, trans. Toshiya Kamei / *Exclusive Artist*

The escape artist slips into the thin transparent cylinder filled with water. With his hands and feet shackled, he begins to fizz.

——

Artista Exclusivo

El escapista se introduce en el reducido y transparente cilindro lleno de agua. Con pies y manos esposados comienza a efervescer.

Sean Hill / *Bemidji in Spring*

In the first city
>> on the eventually
> Mighty Mississippi
ice fishing
> is
>> day-to-day,
> the ice darkening,
green
> like a bruise,
>> according to the locals
—speaking to something
deeper
>> than the lake. Why not
money or envy or leaves in deep summer
or my fancy
> far away
>> from this middle place,
a bit of glass,
broken wine bottle say,
> cast overboard at sea
>>> green against blue
>> tumbling
> back
to shore
a frosted shard
because I don't
bruise that way.
At any rate it shrinks,
>> melting from the edges, becoming
an island to which the gulls
return, shrieking with spring.

Eunsong Kim / *The Car*

You took my hand to have me seated next to you in a small almost golden-
    colored car
And I saw a country pass with words with the soft elimination of an argu-
    ment that put freeways on my feet

There was nothing in my purse or my pockets
nothing in my eyes 'for me to catch you'

        Sometimes I sleep with the doors unlocked so please tell me

if love is the last thing you seek

Gareth Lee / *Eulogy*

my lungs of eucalypt, my lungs have taken in

wincing like iron
as the earth deploys birds as
it wheels they vanish

Point to the part
that says "x," on the breastbone or hip
Point to the open

the standing invitation with legs
maimed and sap
laid on wounds, or make

pronounce a farewell
say I am too reckless to keep

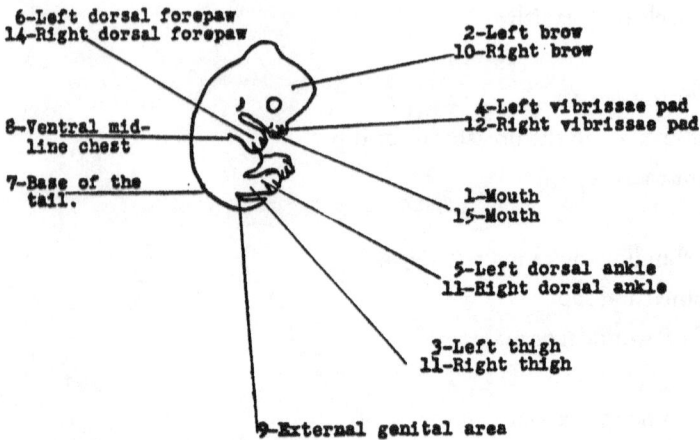

6-Left dorsal forepaw
14-Right dorsal forepaw

2-Left brow
10-Right brow

4-Left vibrissae pad
12-Right vibrissae pad

8-Ventral mid-
line chest

7-Base of the
tail.

1-Mouth
15-Mouth

5-Left dorsal ankle
11-Right dorsal ankle

3-Left thigh
11-Right thigh

9-External genital area

FIG 1. THE FIFTEEN STIMULUS POINTS USED SHOWN ON THE RIGHT SIDE OF A 12 MM. FETUS

Matt Leibel / *The Island*

Here are some of the things that were found on the island: a ball of twine; a 1/10000 scale model of the Sistine Chapel made out of seaweed; a half-eaten grapefruit; the eight of clubs from a deck of nudie cards; a ruffled paper plate slathered with French fry grease; a ring of interlocking paper clips wide enough to fit around the neck of a lion; a wallet full of Albanian currency and the business card of a Tiranese magician and/or musician (the card was wet and blurry); a treasure map; a solid gold baseball stuffed inside a coconut buried under sand deep inside a seaside cave; a green magic potion reputed to give the imbiber a one in ten chance at immortality (we won't know how this pans out till later); a letter to the Sultan of Brunei signed by a woman named Claudia de Passolini, the former hostess of an Italian television program on which people have various of their body parts turned into molds and made into truffle-filled chocolates; a famous painting of a famous photograph, which photograph depicts a painting of a photograph, and so forth in a kind of endless Escheresque progression; a kangaroo, whose pouch doubles as a fax machine; a garden in which giant asparagus grow so high they reach the sun, then grow right through the sun as though skewering it; a species of frog whose facial features change depending on who or what is looking at it; a map of the island as imagined by mapmakers who had themselves never visited but had had the island lovingly described to them over the phone (this is the most accurate map of the island extant to date); a teardrop the size of a small child (speculation about the creature who cried it leading to a lonely monster residing in the same cave where the gold-baseball-stuffed-inside-a-coconut also resides); a message in a washed-ashore bottle that reads: "Sorry, Try Again"; several sticks lined up along the beach arranged to read RESCUE ME, followed several yards further on by more sticks lined up to read JUST KIDDING I LIKE IT HERE AND GOING HOME SEEMS TOO SCARY NOW; a non-fiction book about comets purportedly written by an actual comet, whose previous book (according to the jacket copy) was more of a psychological thriller, though also about comets (i.e. the effect on the residents of a small New England fishing village when struck by a comet); another monster, this one female, who apparently lives in the cave with the first monster, and who, the pair of them, are in the midst of a messy divorce; a musical instrument entirely made from bamboo with strings fashioned out of stray electrical wiring found amidst the wreckage of the small plane that crashed here around 1997; an increasingly hairy and long-bearded human being who has forgotten his name (it is Mike Davidson) who strums the instrument (it is a harp) in an attempt to lure the dueling monsters out from their cave in order that he can retrieve the solid-gold baseball (a parting gift from his former professional team, upon his retirement as a professional baseball pitcher back in 1989, honoring his 300 minor league wins) he had hidden in the cave soon after the plane crash; a Virginia Slims cigarette in the mouth of the male monster, who had taken up smoking only after several crates of cigarettes washed ashore years before; a weathered tan baseball glove that fits snugly around the four-fingered right hand of the female monster, who is, just now, tossing the solid gold baseball against the wall of the cave and fielding grounders; a response, by the male monster, to the tune being played on the bamboo harp by Mike "Minnesota Masher" Davidson, in the form of the monster's decision to step outside the cave for the first time in several years; a response to the response, in the form of the female monster (whose name is Bellaguizzin) following her soon-to-be-ex-husband (whose name is Parabogoragak) outside the cave, baseball still in hand; a pen, bearing the address and phone number of the Minnesota Twins front office, in the front paw of the kangaroo, who is jotting down an account of these events on the back of Claudia De Passolini's letter to the Sultan of Brunei (which, incidentally, expresses her undying love for the Sultan, who has hundreds of other lovers, a fact she well knows, in all likelihood) and is faxing said account, via his pouch, directly to the office at my Marina Del Rey beach house; a negotiation, between Mike Davidson and the two married-but-estranged monsters, which starts with Mike Davidson offering the monsters 1.5 million Albanian lek in exchange for the solid gold baseball (they could keep the coconut); a confrontation, following the failed negotiation, in which Mike Davidson attempts to fell the two monsters by pelting them with the bottle and sticks lined up on the sand; a slaying, in which the monsters, who can breathe fire (did I mention earlier the monsters can breathe fire?) char Mike Davidson to a crisp; a reconciliation, between Bellaguizzin and Parabogoragak, who were both so ancient and venerable they could barely remember what had caused the strife between them in the first place; a tsunami, subsuming all of the above to underwater oblivion, excepting one small, test tube vial containing the green immortality potion, which washes up on shore outside my beach house, and which I drink quickly and then immediately find myself wondering, do I really want to live forever, do I, in a world in which the island no longer exists?

Genine Lentine / *My Father's Comb*

Black plastic
raised letters
proclaimed it
unbreakable
and so I began
to bend the un-
relenting spine.
First nothing,
then a little give,
heat at the seam,
blanching
at the faultline.
Half an hour
at his mirror, I
worked at it.
I worked it away
from me and
back. I worked
at the word
until the word,
until the atom
of its lie split,
until the word
broke in my hands.

Interview with the Pear Tree

When did you start making pears?

What is a pear?

(She runs her fingers over one
hanging on the branch.)

Mmm. Yes. It began
before I could be seen,
when the great body rang,
striking, for the first time, the earth.
Over the long day, it lay in the sun,
and the birds came, and the flesh
fell away until all that was left
was the seed. Maybe it was
when the moon swelled
the seed, maybe
when the first true
leaf quickened.

Did you always know you would make pears?

I wouldn't know how not to.

What is your process?

I let the leaves
come to the branch
and when the bee is at the
blossom, I listen.

Is dormancy difficult?

    Dormancy?

A period when nothing happens.

    (The tree pauses.)
    I've never had one.

What about drought?

    I spread my root hairs and wait.

Do you ever doubt?

    When the bud breaks the green wood.

Do you ever think of making apples?

    What is an apple?

Could you describe the kind of pears you make?

    (A ripe pear drops into her upturned hands.)

Carlo Matos / *The Little Summer: Physics, Love, and Moving*

When we moved in July, it cut everything in half.
Our old friend, in his grief, carried with him his rusty razor
trying to divide his morning cereal,
his noon-time sun,
and his evening reading.
We were a Higgs Boson—
a catchy phrase for an impossibly complex idea.
Without us his beard grew raucous,
and his face was bloody from the hacking.
It was all very embarrassing.
It was a line of sand—
without width or depth—
and yet we continued to measure the heaps:
one represented before
the other, predictably, after.
The more we swept, the worse it got.
The little summer, one half collapsing into the other—
a singularity again—if they exist—
was our best result:
Wavering.

Here. _____ Here.

And—

Here.

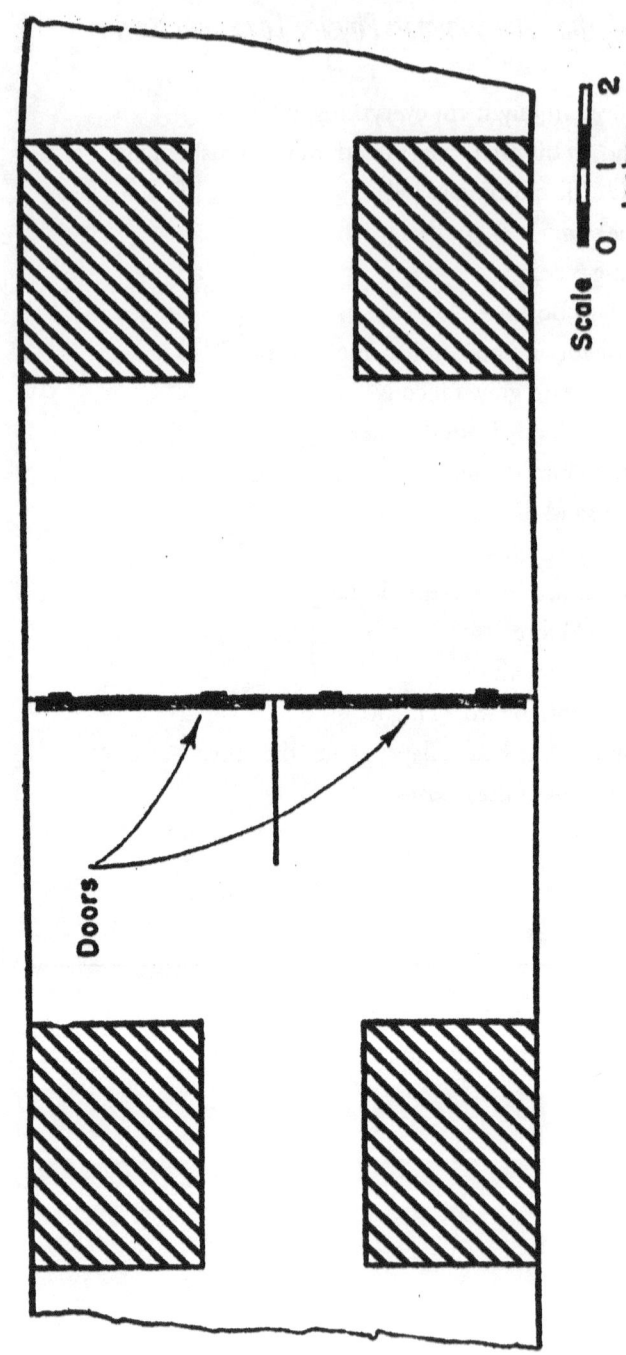

Fig. 1. Top View of One Unit of Maze

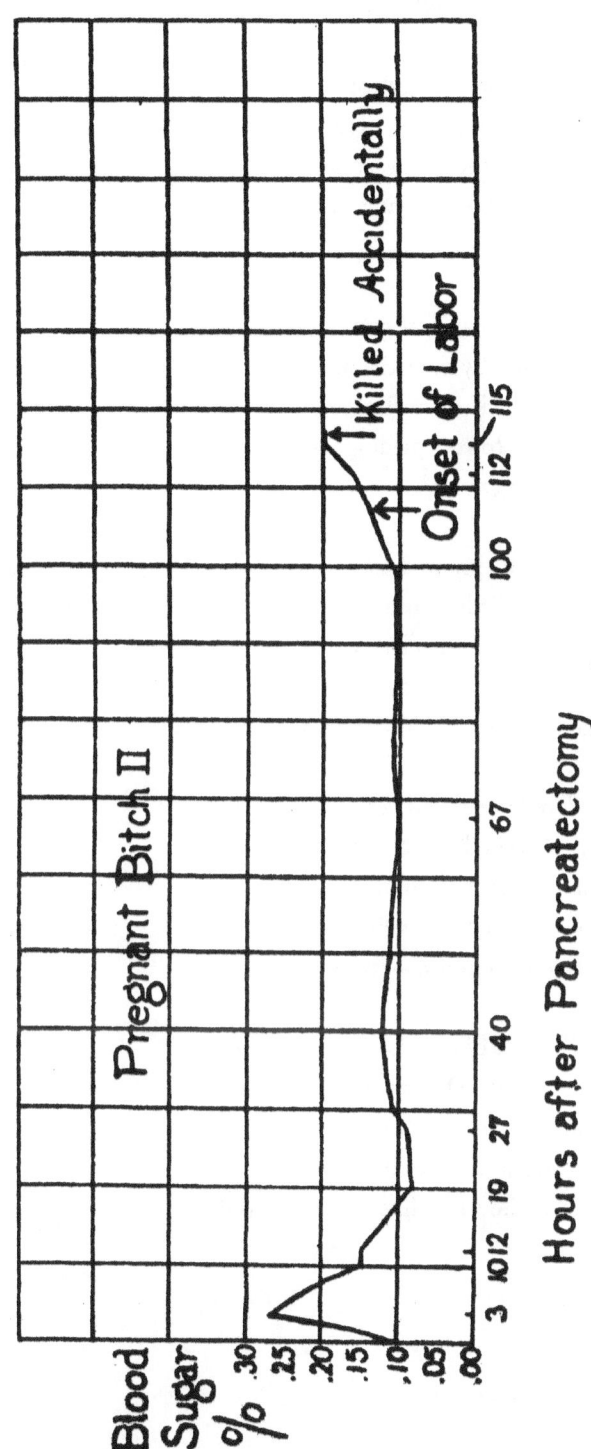

Kyle McCord / *Monotheism*

little number, how sweet you
were to me! all night you bled
your calm into the wet wash
of mud and lotus sickening along
the riverline.

you awoke in a heave of dust,
knocked about by men, drunk
with an oily luck. an anchor
tipped its hat to you, girding itself
before a kiel sky, an algae skin,

and the ax who granted us
a second star. little number,
your body flaked with wet sand,
you suffered every constellation,
scourged yourself in the desert.

were offered bread and fed
with winnowed flecks of rust.
your hair, a beautiful auburn,
was tamped beneath a veil till
you rotted into sinews of muscle.

before the eyes of priests, little
number, you were bound. the bindings
thick, and smelling of horsehair,
you strained a single arm to scratch
at our faces, hovering like a hungry mask.

Marc McKee / At the Edge of a Deep, Dark Wood, Re-Purposed Dolphin Speaks

The they it almost always is
      want to catapult obsolete delivery trucks, elastic plastics,
any extra modern &c into the atmosphere's faults,

the they whose blueprints and schematics whirligig
      so beautifully and fatally
through the softer parts becoming lately late.

           Lately I am desiring my god-effect
      but I fear I have had already my god-effect,

a squeak, click, brush of air so someone has the sense of being kissed
      or whispered intensely to just before they woke.
Just as a toe makes a delicious curve

in the saturated sand before the wilderness of the sea,
      so we move in the air of this world
which will cover the dent we made when we leave.

           O, our fortress is on five kinds of fire
      but until such expirations as we make

should we not move forward at a keening kneel
      of course already? yes quite thank you here
take my hand. *Fin.* Should we not advance

much celebrant in the throes of nothing
      as in the fantasias of love, budging, stuttering,
gainsaying the fearful knives sketching into the vitalia?

Sure. Convince me. I say the knives are fearful
which is why they are sharp.

Today men who were once
        boys mottling backyards with firecrackers, boys
with equations starring their eyeglasses,

who calculated the vectors of forces diverse
        even being pushed down stairs
are saying *Save the world!* via

                the shooting of stuff into the stratosphere.
        Half a world and 17 degrees of hunger away

a detective soldiery rifles the graveyard
        of a despot's toy box and discovers
a yet-to-be-assembled supergun. At this stage

it is unweird for a dolphin to shimmy loose
        from the approved blossoms
bedecking the mini-mall

                at the edge of a deep, dark wood.
        Now we are certain

we have made too much mention of light,
        now we know we will never be able
to have mentioned it enough.

A poison glides severely
        from each motion we make.
Nothing has ever been this good.

                How else paint the world

but with devouring fire, how else live

                    but running with rickshaws full of ice?
      and as one swift and elegant, moving

under the impossible, darling weight of an ocean.

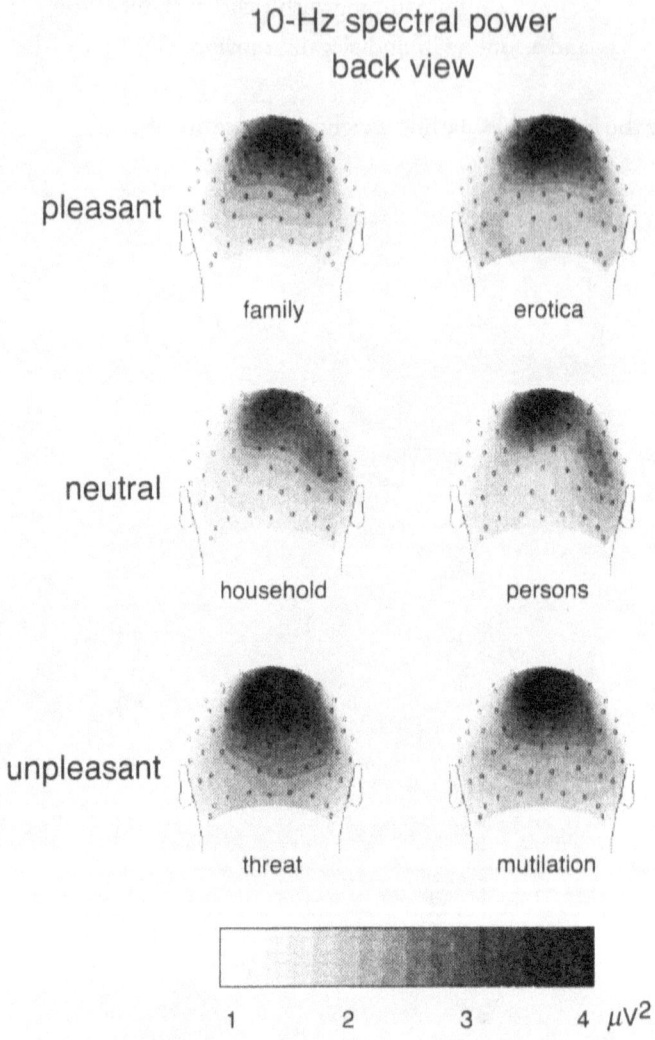

Figure 6. Grand mean ($n = 19$) spline-interpolated topographical distribution of 10-Hz spectral power for six specific contents. A back view is shown.

Ben Mirov / *Hider Roser*

You want to write about a horse
but you have written hose. Think of meat.
Meat thinking of jogging.
Meat going out on a date to see the water.
The water is beautiful and she allows you
to put your arm around her.
Smell her ear, part of a star
that exploded when you were negative
10,000 years old. It smells like vanilla.
In a few hours she is gone.
In four years, even goner
and Dan is telling you something about nothing
the sparrows in his tattoo
forever flying out of a rose
until Dan is dead.
Pretty soon you have a loft
and people are getting to know your work
rearranging the letters in horse rider
to get hider roser, which means something
you will never understand
with only a few minutes left
one end of the hose going into your head the other
going don't know where

The Braille of Evenings is Written in Poem

I stare out of my window with a flashlight behind each eye.
I do not know what I am looking for.
The bushes barely quiver in the wind.
A few people get into a mauve truck.
I return to my couch.
Darkness creeps into the corners of the microwave.
A river disappears into a plastic coffee cup.
I pet a moth as big as a baby.
The desert approaches
inch by ecstatic inch.
What did the lamp say?
Permission to drink ink from the sink?
I feel a vineyard growing inside me.
No need to be alarmed.
Shut the door. Glass of wine. Try to sleep.
My eucalyptus grove can hardly breathe.
Memories of pagoda duck-pond relief.
Diode, diode, nomenclature.
Nocturne for Susie.
The people return to the apartment complex.
Their suits and ties are torn to shreds.
Their cars are barely audible songs.
A grizzly bear snags a salmon made of dreams.
I remove the duct tape from my naked body.
If the sun comes up
I won't be a different person.

I is to Vorticism

as red leaves are to riverbanks.
As American History is to blackout drunk.
As blackout drunk is to flying away.
If you come upon a vortex in your laundry tonight
don't be afraid.
Give it a name like Scheherazade.
Take it to dinner,
feed it oysters and champagne.
They don't teach you this in college
or how to deal with moving faster than the speed of light
into a brick wall,
but that's how I got my diploma
knocking around in the chrysalis
until they pulled me out
and the figment in my wings dried
and my tongue refused to bifurcate.
Mighty big snow-globe head.
Mindful of harmless laser beams.
Three or four ideas spinning around a coat hanger.
Lasso after lasso.

|

Trey Moody / *The Seating*

Blue chair on its plastic back. Grass
and its green leaning
                         toward the dirt. More
is what we've wanted, and now—
a cue from the trees: consider the security
of your silences. Forget.
          Listen when the earth becomes self-aware
and take the red chair in your hand, set it
on the ground; sit down.

Mark Neely / *Ten Year Tunnel*

Everything I do is disappointing. I was moving on just fine, Elvis Costello on the radio, when the road curved into a sudden tunnel and the sun blazed out like flash paper.

Rimbaud said we must get high, lest we start believing in the world. But cigarettes trashed my lungs until I had to quit, and when I drink the porchlight throws fuzz around the house, electric hair. To what world-gristle does coffee wake me?

I lay these bricks forever, only for the sun to do them in.

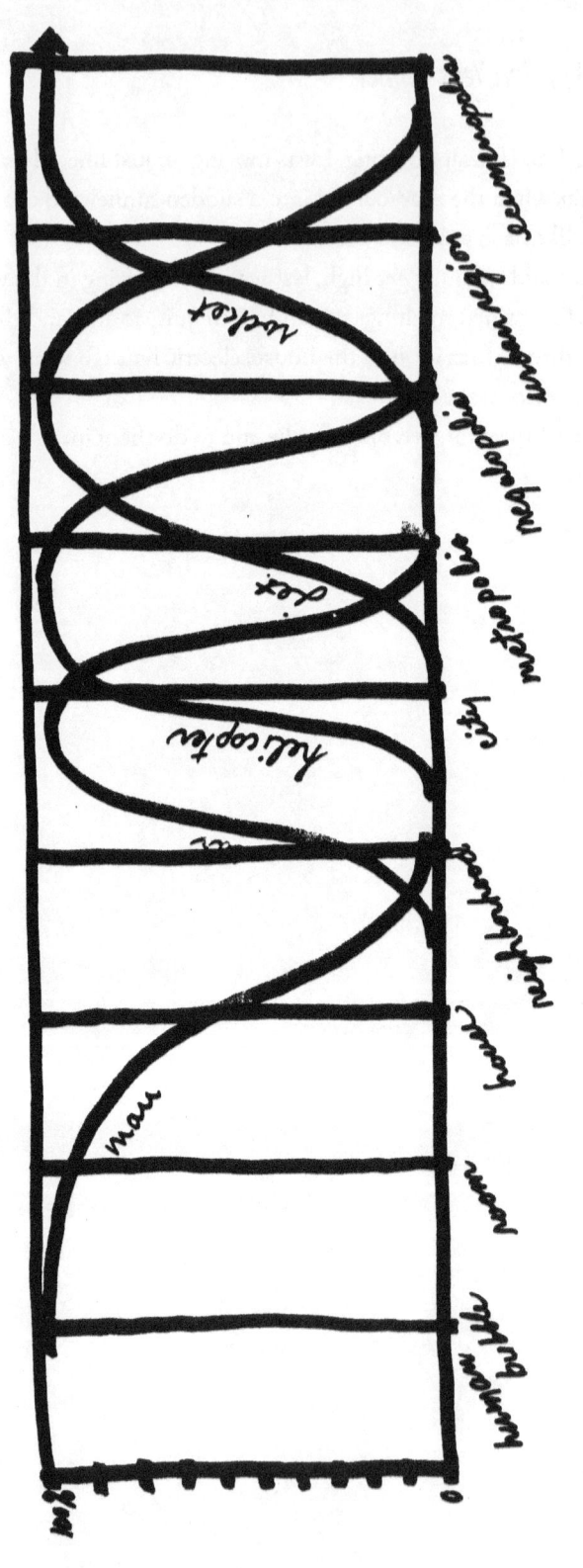

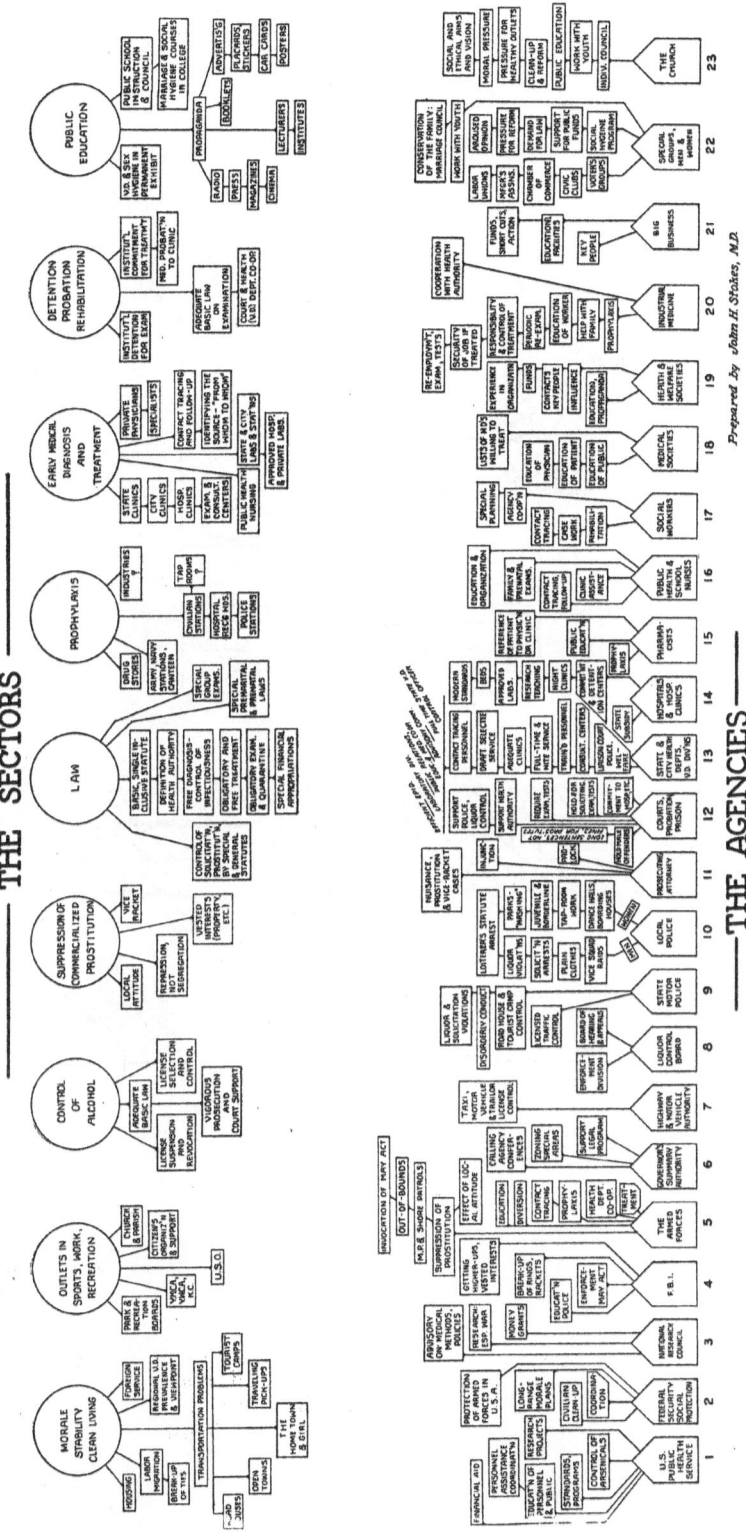

Fig. 876.—A blueprint of venereal disease control.

Prepared by John H. Stokes, M.D.

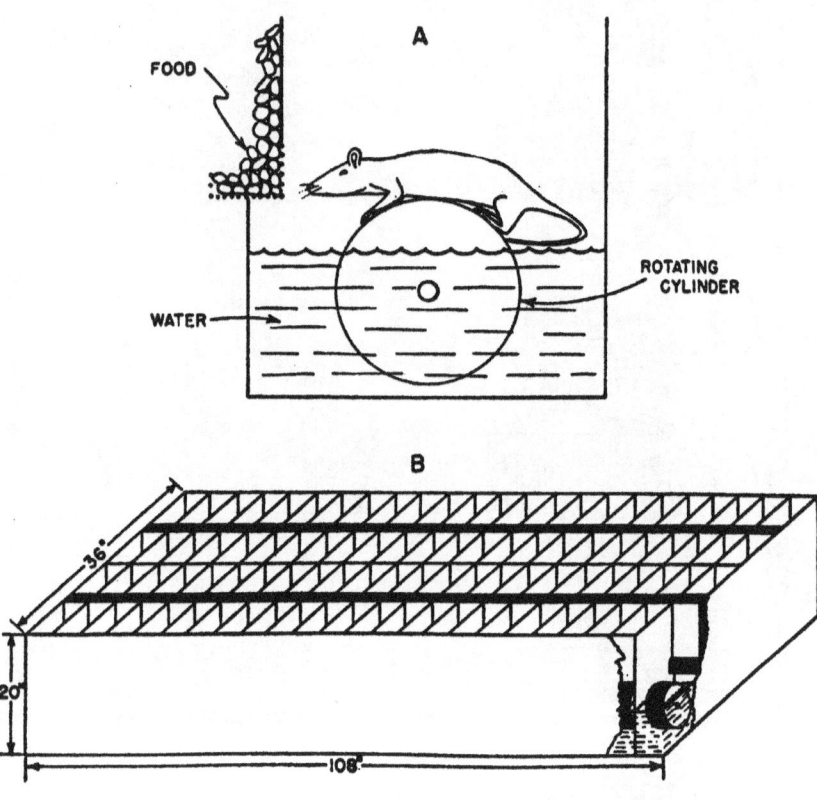

FIG. I

FIG. 1. Apparatus Used to Enforce Wakefulness

Amy Newman / *3 Poems*

DIAGRAM c/o Ander Monson
Dept of English, PO Box 210067
University of Arizona
Tucson, AZ 85721-0067

1 January

Dear Editor:

Please consider the enclosed poems for publication with *Diagram*. They are from my manuscript, X = *Pawn Capture*, a lyrical study of chess as we played it in my family: the first move has to take place while everyone is thinking about something other than chess. For my grandparents diversion was love, and between his rage-filled checkmates and her play dates with saints, they braided my teenage years spent mostly schooling and listening and keeping the house free of insects.

When in our backyard caterpillars mastered the flowering dogwoods, and our neighbor rapped on the trees with a stick to disperse them, her image reminded my grandmother of Hortense tormenting Germana Cousin for her presumed pilfering of a small loaf of bread. Germana opens her dress and her saintliness is revealed as summer flowers tumble out in a herald of love and beauty. Here my grandmother saw chastisement and the Holy Hand of her Invisible Lord Partitioning The Mortals with some tiny visuals about The Power and The Glory but I thought if so He was really Just Sprinkling the World with His Blossoms and Berries, and if Germana's cottons could give way to an onrush of flesh, abandoning its pinks and greens and holy stamens and anthers and spilt maple leaves and maybe even ruffles of filaments and pollen, might it ever be under my opened dress, this mound of petals, with my thin body lighter than bone from what I knew? So when I looked up and the neighbor was walking away over broken dogwood blossoms snowing down, I wished hard for a language that would tell you of this beautiful sight which I have never before seen, not even on a holy card, and this in spite of my grandmother's hissing at our neighbor and retrieving a rake. I spent the afternoon carrying away the remainders of Germana's undressing and tried to find a dictionary I could bring to my room. Because *beautiful* is a word that my workshop class says is ineffective, that it doesn't contain how this sight captures my attention and convinces me, absorbs and converts me away from the yard, so that the closest kin might be *diverting*, which the class might find archaic, and if that's true, then I don't know how to say that everything in the backyard might be pretending to be lovely in order that we can all get up in the morning.

Thank you for your consideration, and for reading. I have enclosed an SASE, and look forward to hearing from you.

Sincerely,
Amy Newman

DIAGRAM c/o Ander Monson
Dept of English, PO Box 210067
University of Arizona
Tucson, AZ 85721-0067

15 December

Dear Editor:

Please consider the enclosed poems for publication with *Diagram*. They
are from my manuscript, *X = Pawn Capture*, an exploration of how my
grandfather used chess as a way to divert a child's attention from the
absence of love between her grandparents and my attempts to capture
in language their magnificent silences, which could have been visitations
from ethereal beings for all they told me.

The pawns on the chessboard are workers, hard workers who get no
thanks in this life, as my grandfather would explain. That's why there are
more pawns than any other pieces, because life is hard and tiring, and
they suffer, and are sacrificed, so that the community can continue and the
game can be played. I would like to see the knight protect a pawn once in
a while, especially a girl pawn, who has let her hair down the long side of a
castle and allowed him to climb up its vermillion border. But my grandfa-
ther tells me that a girl pawn would be run out of town on a rail because
she would be nothing but trouble, a bee in the bonnet of the community
with her frills and her soft skins and the hiding of the special areas, and
the Queen, of all pieces, would see to it that any young lady who came
calling even to remark *what a cold day we have!* or *how are you doing kind
sir?* would not last long, he might say while watching my grandmother
peel from an eternal mound of onions one large and stubborn skin that
unrolled only in bits and flakes.

But if the girl pawn *was* trapped in the castle piece and the knight watched
her sighing, day after day, I think then that even the chokeberries that the

birds devoured outside our windows on these cold days might instead stay in their first, pure, flowery blooms, so impressed the space outside our house would be by the atmosphere of real high school love, and not whatever it was that made the boy who was trying out for the football team stare from the corner of our street as I stumbled away like a spent insect after a curious and feeble forced embrace, lips entirely embarrassed and neck dismayed at his scratchy growth that assaulted, rearranging my shirts and skirts which were only pulled at a little but when I got home and undressed in my room, my blouse would refuse to crumple in a heap that didn't look compromising. And outside my window no steadfast knight, who would rather die than force his hands down the open collar of my blouse and giggle while his knees pressed and pried like a tweezers. No knight outside in the cold air awaiting with glistening eyes by the choke-cherries, sighing, or anyone interested in seeing if my hair, now gleaming and yellow and strong as steel, would lift them to some noble cause. In the kitchen my grandmother tore at the spice leaves, and in the main room my grandfather remained, forever irritated at chess.

Thank you for your consideration, and for reading. I have enclosed an SASE, and look forward to hearing from you.

Sincerely,
Amy Newman

DIAGRAM c/o Ander Monson
Dept of English, PO Box 210067
University of Arizona
Tucson, AZ 85721-0067

29 March

Dear Editor:

Please consider the enclosed poems for publication with *Diagram*. They
are from my manuscript, $X = Pawn\ Capture$, and you know all about it.
Like everything else n the world, as I deduce from probability class and
statistics and beauty, the paths we make with our little bodies through this
universe half-real, half-jellied like summer sherbet, are small but signifi-
cant. I might make a comparison with the pretty marks a chicken's foot
makes in the scratch, or the way a low bending pine branch will write on
spring mud, patiently, in the quiet March wind. And that's what's going
on now. The tree branch is weighed down from the thaws, nodding and
moving the wet dirt, and I am here, writing to you, while my grandmother
stands in her boots and coat, burning another stack of mail. I recognize
the stamps on the envelopes, of course. From this distance and in her
winter coat, I might mistake grandmother for Euphrosyne, the saint who
renounced her possessions, dressed as a man, and for years instructed
her own father in the spiritual life, until she revealed herself and her own
father broke into blossoms and shook with truth. But above the burning
and the smoke of the metal bin where your replies are smoldering is the
kind and shining face of Teresa, reading the ash, and a stunning bundle of
pale green petals, and many, many, patterning birds. I wish you could see
this.

Thank you for your consideration, and for reading. I have enclosed an
SASE, and look forward to hearing from you.

Sincerely,
Amy Newman

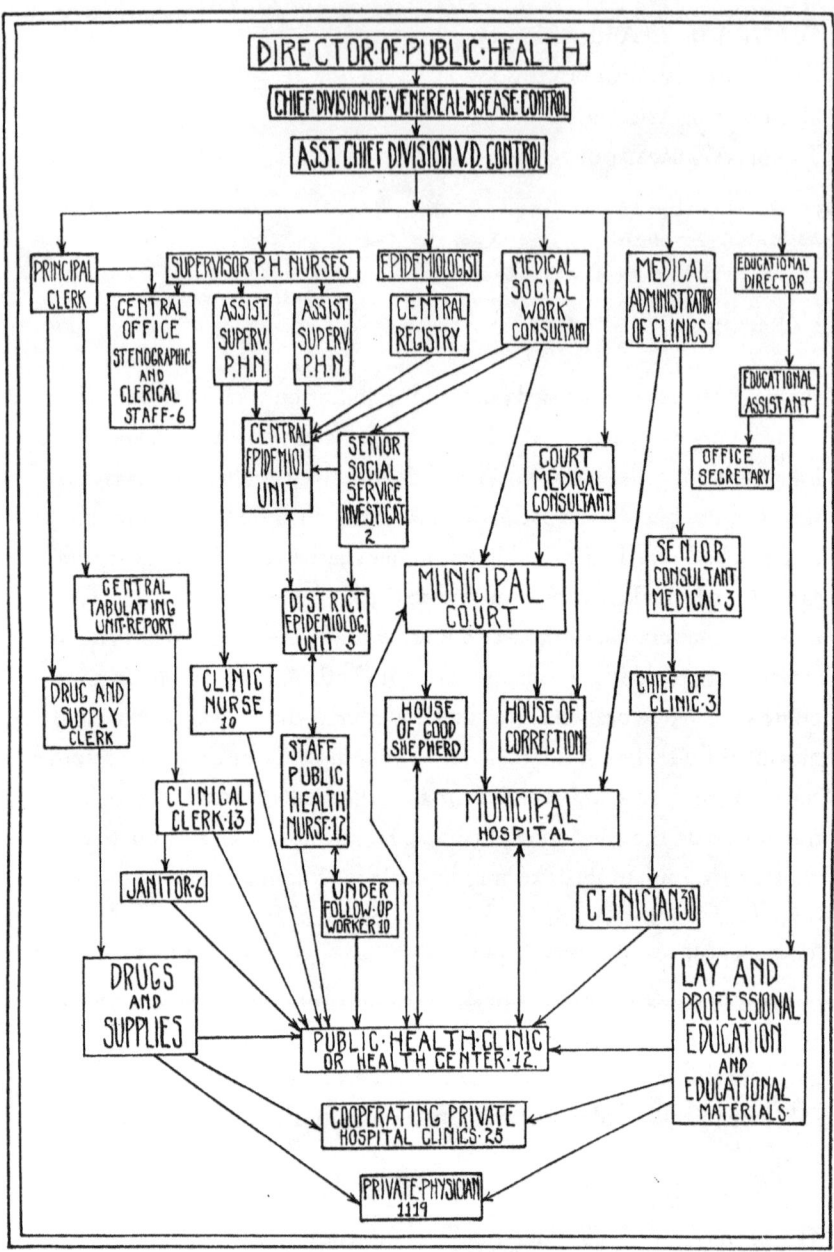

Fig. 878.—Organizational Chart of a City Department of Public Health Venereal Disease Control Program. The arrows indicate the directions of supervision or service from the central administrative office. Numerals within the squares show the number of locations or the strength of the staff in each position as the case may be. This is based upon the 1943–44 budget of the City of Philadelphia Venereal Disease Control Division with staff of 113 full time and part time individuals and an annual expenditure of approximately ten cents per capita as outlined in the text on p. 1202.

JoAnna Novak / *Holiday Sestina with Zombies*

Wherein I'll chew calcified dainties & address
my recent proclivity for living the dead, home
grown & headband-bound with those white
gauze guides to life: a bit unfit, a little
too lascivious—*she wanted, she suffered*—
throats & apertures, composed & shot.

I mean, just look at her. There's bloodshot
eyes & that unraveling ravishment, undressing
all hours of the night, raised rumor-suffering,
café curtains studded with blood-red homes.
One at a time, the living start to look a little
more like a box of unmentionables. White

between the fingers, racing hearts gulping white
air—when it's invisible, it's all the rage, one shot
to test her tolerance for analgesics, days littered
with useful secrets & *let's get boned* dressed
up like other people. One night we stayed home,
got a little high, & she orgasmed into suffering.

No one ate pineapple or crullers. We just suffered
through a can of peaches in syrup, tap water white-
clouded & tinny. The movie where the lady's home
vendettas act in curious ways: the animals are shot
standing. The tulips ooze yellow pus. Boys dressed
for debauch, delirious in the datura & just a little

too dreamy-eyed over leaving Christchurch sans little
trumpets, spiny fruit, & a single evening of sexless suffering
in the bush. It was one of those nights without address,
landmark, or catcall & she launched into lording white

elephants out back—but, then maybe my shot's
off, maybe she was dishabille & crumby, homesick

for one roomful of revenants. This was the last home
without sores. The prize driveway, scoured-shoal, lit
by luminaries. She said *time's right for God's shot
glass.* Our final holiday season pre-price suffering
adjustments, gifted malaise—a lot of pearly whites
bared amidst a village haunting where undressing

addresses our homes of Christmas past,
little white doves arcing through golden
velum shot with starburst punches & suffering.

Brian Oliu / *C:\Run Penelope.exe*

The x is on the other y, incorrect addresses create incorrect maps, the cartographer stuck in traffic somewhere, elsewhere, on the back of busses, hands gripping metal to ground self from the electric shock, how walking across carpet can cause memory to short circuit, the same action causing hair to stand on end after scuffing balloons on basement rugs; it is a blessing to be without analog, ironically letting magnets and point-of-sale hardware doing all of the work, to unlatch bolts and swing open breezeways, no turn of key, turn of phrase, simple turning of crashing systems over, once, twice, as sides and limbs get too warm, skin on shoulder grows taught to close up pores ineffectively boxing out cooling rooms where towers hum. The instruction pointer sequences the inverse of thermonuclear reactions, neglecting the spreading of hues on ice caps north of here (wherever here may be), which would reduce albedo, salt and dirt on sidewalks, clumping together like threshold levels stuck at 128, but you'd never travel that north, east maybe, west perhaps, south certainly, as I know beyond reason you were there, and I saw you mixing chemicals to ascertain mixed chemicals that cause glasses hurled across laminated coffins with coasters and late night excuses perched upon the symbolic dead. I saw

```
APPLICATION ERROR PENELOPE.EXE CAUSED A GEN-
ERAL PROTECTION FAULT IN MODULE OLIU.EXE AT
0001:1122B NO CHILDREN TO BE SAVED FROM LAC-
ERATIONS, NO GLIMMERS, JUST ANOMALOUS CONDI-
TIONS, THE STORING OF MEMORY BEYOND OUR BOUNDS
```

```
C:\run penelope.exe
```

The x is on the other y, the bouncing of spindled trees to red rocks, vortexes created to bring serenity in other-wise gridded spaces, no time for open energy to spin, just the bouncing off of financial districts and revised flaxmills, Hooke's law be damned if springing back is possible. Home is not home, dollar slices shunned, three-dollar cans shunned, brooding now, brooding. Hands with no rings in wool pockets, leather pressed to skin sides, and it's not even cold there; the rigidness of security measures to keep overweening suitors from breaking down doors, or at least sliding through them sideways like shuffled punch cards. I picture

```
APPLICATION ERROR PENELOPE.EXE CAUSED A GEN-
ERAL PROTECTION FAULT IN MODULE OLIU.EXE AT
0001:1122B NO GANGS OF HUNTERS, NO LIONS CIR-
CLING, JUST THE OVERWRITING OF DATA OUTSIDE OF
LINES OF ALLOCATED OVERWRITING
```

```
C:\run penelope.exe
```

The x is on the other y, the move away from barcodes to prevent photo-copies to magnets, black stripes, the unification of access levels, as there are places where we can access together, % start sentinel, and that's where the similarities end. It used to be simple; saw to metal on the streets, or holes in plastic. All things now considered and all things encrypted, password protected, a serial of serials, integers and alphabetics both, glyphs maybe, a sequence of sequences. For 128 alternate between capital letters, lower case letters, letters written and never returned (shift enter to return) and numbers, numbers never received. Names of dogs found dead on the side of suburban roads, monikers escaped from with a new postal address, children crushed by steering wheels and their anticipated date of gradua-tion, favorite foods, inside jokes between estranged lovers, maiden names. As it stands, a series of asterisks, placeholders for the authentication and authorization, and this, the auditing of

```
APPLICATION ERROR PENELOPE.EXE CAUSED A GEN-
ERAL PROTECTION FAULT IN MODULE OLIU.EXE AT
0001:1122B NO CUNNING RINGS, NO FINISHING NO
NO NO Sleeping, Brian Oliu, your heart so
wrung with sorrow? No need, I tell you, no,
```

the MEGA-MIGHTY GODS who live at ease can't
bear to let you ERROR

```
C:\run penelope.exe -safe
```

SAFEMODE Single-user mode, no daemons, a place for root users no
auto executives, 16-bit 640x480 drifting softly at the gate, chandeliers in
cars, extended guestbooks and logs in front of touch screens, apples and
genuflecting. Phantoms, all, all in spun-sugar dresses with fox patterns.
The luckless man; is he still alive? Does he see the light of day? Or is he
dead already, lost in the House of Death?

"About that man," she says, transparent as she arrives, "All tools that cut
and divide things in half signify disagreements, factions, and injuries.
I cannot tell you the story start to finish, whether he's dead or alive. It's
wrong to lead you on with idle words." At that she ascended and descend-
ed off by the doorpost past the bolt; gone on a lifting and sinking breeze,
axis mundi perpendicular, up and under.

Figure 2

CONSTRAINTS AND LIMITS OF STRUCTURE

Kim Parko / *Cliques for the Dead*

When we were little, we died of broken bones. All of our bones shattered inside us. They came out as dust through our mouths and ears. They came out as dust between our legs. They came out as dust through our pores. What was left in our bodies was connective tissue. We were filled with connective tissue that had nothing to connect. This was the cause of our deaths. We were buried on Cloud Top Hill. The funerals were neat and small and the wakes were dry. When we died, we came up to the top of Cloud Top Hill before our funerals. We could see all the layers of the worlds superimposed on one another. We could not pick out our world among them, but we could find pieces. We eventually saw our caskets; they shimmered in and out of being. We were glad, now, that our bones had come out. We were suppler, and in death we could exist without bones. Living people called us ghosts—the way we could fit through a keyhole. We could talk to each other. We were glad we had died together. We could see other people that died. We could talk to them, but everybody liked the people that they died with best. The cliques of the dead are somewhat like the cliques of the living, but they are less superficial.

Shelia and Hector

Shelia was born in the year of the branch. Hector was born in the year of
the boat. Shelia and Hector met on a subway train. Shelia spoke first, ten-
tatively, to the passenger beside her, "where are you going?" Hector replied,
"to a jungle island." Shelia was not aware of a jungle island anywhere close
to the city. She knew where the tentacles of the subway stretched. "How
will you get there?" she asked. "I have chartered this ship to sail there."
Shelia was alarmed to note that the ship he spoke of was the subway train.
Hector began the motions of a seaman: unfurling sails, knotting ropes,
and finding his bearings. Shelia thought about the jungle. She would
be among her own there. She examined her twigs, already round with
buds. She imagined another year of wasted pollen, of the gentle yellow
cloud that fell from her, only to be assailed by street sweepers. Shelia's sap
coursed with intent. She looked out the window of the subway train to
see a school of mackerel gliding by, their backs shimmering beneath the
surface.

Adam Peterson / *The Flasher Calls His Mother.*

Weather jobs lunch someday jobs. His tired diaphragm coughs up up-words. This sounds like good. This sounds like goodbye-love. They share mornings gone sunny. And afternoons gone night. Birds get a job hot out stars stars moon. Tomorrow, again.

Figure 82. Double-Drowning Release (in Position).
Figure 83. Double-Drowning Release (Leverage Applied).

Figure 84. Double-Drowning Release (Victims Separated).

Cecilia Pinto / *Green Girls Villanelle*

The other one dreaming
flutter, come and whisper
two green girls all deep and meaning

unseen mountains always moving.
If you are her
the other one is dreaming

of white petal pink, flowers seeming
to deep kiss your mouth. Ask them to linger.
Two green girls all deep and meaning

yellow fish flash in the river streaming.
Moss cleaves to stones, and what do you, what do you
if one was dreaming

of brown wood, blue meadow? See
red deer rut in the open air.
Hear two green girls all deep and meaning

the rain is heavy, wet and clean.
Can you be thicket, be arbor, be bower
to the other one's dreaming?
Two green girls all deep and meaning.

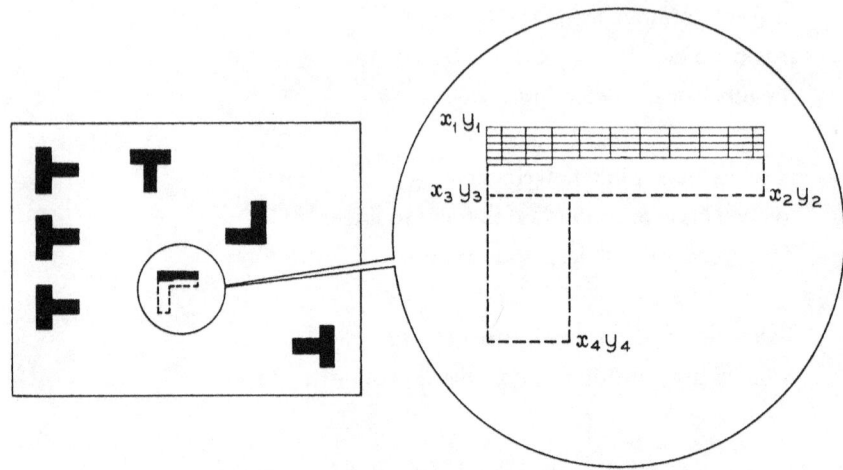

Fig. 2—Method of filling blocks using line segments.

Lia Purpura / Why Some Hybrids Work and Others Don't

The chili-chocolate gelato didn't work because the chili numbed my mouth, as did the cold—and all that activity canceled out the chocolate.

Cockapoos and Labradoodles work well for owners, but they really hack off the breeders whose business is promoting and maintaining singularity. I'm sure the dogs are nice (and really, what's not to like in Labs and Poodles and big-eyed Spaniels) but for me, they don't work because the names are dumb and make perfectly dignified animals sound like toys. Of course, we, who have a standard poodle, also irk breeders since we refused to have her tail docked and she has no haircut to speak of. Most people assume she's a Labradoodle. I can see it's hard to be a breeder.

The wild yellow trim on the staid, dark green house down the street could've worked, but then my neighbor went and used a different yellow on the door and now everything clashes. The problem here is consistency—not the wild-domestic hybrid itself. For example, satyrs work—one end is all thoughtful and conversant, the other, all animal-action. *I'm not sure exactly how they work.* Nymphs would know best. But I do know, in a satyr, the wild part stays wild, the cultivated part stays cultivated. Satyrs are complicated but consistent. Friends, your best, most redemptive love won't change a satyr.

One can buy a hanging indoor/outdoor fixture to serve as either a porch-light or living room light, and if you're undecided, need both, need one temporarily, then that's a good idea. But the halogen office lamp used on the porch, as a porch light: that doesn't work. Many things work in new contexts, but not if their initial purpose dominates. Then porches go makeshifty; then they start looking like scrappy undergrad rentals.

The fig tree in our yard is a hybrid gesture, a combo of Mediterranean botany and Mid-Atlantic desire. (That it was given to us by our Greek friend, Constantine, who's a Japanese historian, is even better). The tree didn't work for two years, but we kept at it, pruning and watering and mulching, because we liked the leaves so much—they were so (we couldn't help it) *Biblical*, and then lo! on the third year the tree took and produced 7 good figs. Sometimes a hybrid gesture takes a long time to root.

Chocolate-covered potato chips worked for me, but not for my friend who likes both chocolate and chips a lot, but couldn't see them together and so didn't even try one. "They don't look right," she said, "the chip is deformed by the chocolate." I felt the chip was reformed, brought back from the edge of way-too-salty, by the good and loving hand of dark chocolate. "It looks like tree lichen," she said. "It tastes like perfect union," I said, "you have no idea what you're missing." My friend is not an "opposites attract" type. Nor does she fancy the syanaesthetic swooning of Nabokov, on whose prose I regularly gorge.

I'm pretty sure that celebrating Christmas and Hannukah together in the same house doesn't really work out. Same with Easter and Passover, though they both share a lamb. Holidays are micro-climates; they greet you at the door and waft and settle. Balsam and ham. Latkes and candle-smoke. Rituals are jealous entities: the hannukah bush, the tree decorated with dreidles—they seem sad and deflated when made to sit nicely next to each other and conjure small talk.

This morning, the ad in the *Baltimore Sun*, for the latest ritzy harbor-side restaurant read: "Max's: A New Tradition." Well, no. That doesn't work. Tradition, I thought, had *something* to do with time.

Mules—the offspring of a male donkey and a female horse—don't "work" in one sense. Neither do hinnies (female donkey and male horse offspring). I mean they don't reproduce. But they *are* real characters. In other words, some hybrid gestures produce singular things. One-time-onlies. Anomalies that are stubborn and ornery. That know their own mind. It might be better to simply enjoy them. At a distance. No use teaching them as "models."

Zebras *look* like hybrids—product of one white and one black horse-like animal—but aren't. The debate rages on (black with white stripes, or white with black stripes) but either way, they're just exactly what you see: a black-and-white beast. Beware the assumed hybrid. In other words, some people are amused to find they write a thing called "the lyric essay" when all along they were just doing what felt natural, simply asserting the sum total of who they are as writers. That no two zebras have the same *pattern* of stripes—now *that's* more interesting, by far.

Starbucks offers a mass of senseless hybrid gestures. Just to start, there's the tyrannical and embarrassing naming system you have to comply with, or risk irritating your barista. Why "tall" and then "grande"? Why "crème" and then "wet" or "dry"? Why "double" and not "doppio?" What's with the random Italianate leanings? Then there's the "you call it/ have it your way" culture that allows for such excesses and hybrid disasters of taste as the "iced decaf, triple grande, no whip soy, five pump, Mocha-mint."

Here's a scene: I am just out of college and back home in NY, working all day, and writing at night, and it's causing the the usual problems. I am in a starkly beautiful sushi bar, eating my one weekly allowance of uni, and drinking my half-price Miller Lite, slowly. It's the roaring, late-80s and one of those baby millionaires sits down next to me and we get to talking. "I'm going to retire at 30 and write a novel," he tells me. He tells me he has "so many ideas." I was tired and righteous and broke. I said something like "nice dream bub, but if you're not doing it *now*, if you don't *need* to do it, it's not gonna happen." I meant, some things have to be there at the outset. I meant—though I wouldn't have said it this way at the time— "You have no drive to hybridize! If you *needed* to write, you'd be, right now, a banker-poet. An insurance guy-novelist. A waiter-playwright. That hyphen would be a little table where you set your work, nightly. A little bridge you crossed, after dinner, to far realms, and crossed back again, in the morning."

If hybrids *fail* because they produce dumb, goofy names, as noted earlier, then they *succeed* when they offer new, sonorous ones. The *pluot*, a hybrid of plum and apricot is lovely. (Ah! hints of "plie" and "Roualt") The *tangelo*'s great (bite in and there's "Tango" and "Angelo" waiting). Not the *papple*, a too-hard, slightly mealy crossing of pear and apple, with the unfortunate echoes of "nipple" and "pimple" and "pap". Not the *peacotum*, a peach/apricot/plum hybrid, with its echoes of "cotyledon." Though it might have been worse. The peacotum's early developer wanted to name the fruit after the nice, soft fuzz it retained, scientifically known as "pubescence" which would have given us—I'm serious now, this was the guy's plan—the "pube-plum." The best thing at the Farmer's Market in Baltimore: the apples. Apples are, a priori, hybrids—or graftings, to be clearer.

Adam and Eve on one side, the power to keep Drs. away on the other My favorites, the Stayman-Winesap and Jonagold, have names that *work*. They indicate fruits that take their essential qualities seriously. They want you to believe in them—not laugh at them. The wine descriptions on the little tags at Well's Discount Liquors in Baltimore are fantastic, and the impulse there, to present taste as an essentially hybridized experience, to be accurate by way of complexity, is right on: Snow and shale, squid and wolf, rose and lichen…forgive me…A.R. Ammons slipped in here—that master of hybrid states of being.

Hybrid tenses work because they help us bend time. Consider the neat and quick gesture the future perfect allows: "By next year/ I will have done X". Such projection and back-tracking rolled into one. I also love the similar veering I undergo when reading certain poems of Marvin Bell that take place in what he calls the "posthumous present."

The hybrid word "Ginormous" works and doesn't. Officially, it's in the new Webster's. Aurally, it's euphonious (whereas the other option, as I figure it—"Enormant"—sounds like a sci-fi bug. And the even more messed up "Enormgi" is wierdly bacterial.) But I don't use the word "Ginormous"—it doesn't work for me, because I'm not 15 and in Jr. High.

Hybrid times of day and night work, *and* have much spiffier names than "day" or "night." On one end there's day-break, dawn, aurora. On the other, twilight, gloaming, crepuscular. Such is the poetry of the liminal dark.

The hybrid car, Prius, works, though not without all kinds of battery problems I hear, and some longer-term problems with toxic disposal. And also it sidesteps the issue of over-consumption, since rationing is likely what we need to do, now and forever—but that's pretty radical. Rationing's un-American. And as of yet, hybrid cars don't have industry backing or any real government muscle behind them. Then again, there are also no accredited MFA programs offering degrees in the prose poem. Thankfully, for the clever, rogue prose poem. Institutionalizing hybrids is complicated.

In a recent letter my novelist friend Kent Meyers described for me the wonders of hybrid corn varieties, whose purposes include increased yield, rootworm and corn borer resistance, early ripening and alkaline soil compatibility. And of the hybrids of his youth, how fondly he recalled the legendary XL-45, the gold standard hybrid for corn farmers in Morgan MN. Is it any wonder that he's just completed his own hybrid, a novel-in-stories (whose title is, by the way, "Twisted Tree")?

So hybrids respond to need, and thus are vital and heightened forms of attention. Consider the split vision and special alertness of the sad kid laughing along with the rest while secretly monitoring jolly, drunk Dad for the first signs of meanness. Or the cop on a date, queued up at the movies—scanning for trouble, mentally noting, annoying his girlfriend who claims he can't ever relax. Or those of us who have trained ourselves to hold one conversation while following a few others at nearby tables in restaurants.

In her memoir *Seeing Through Places*, Mary Gordon writes of her mother's reverence, her love, really, for the priests in their life, and of the priests' mutual deep regard for her mother. One might be tempted to call such love "stunted," "unrequited" or "sad." Or, one might call up the term "passionate restraint." That's a hard one…love is, whose origins are mysterious, whose success requires odd and challenging integrations, whose future is always surprising.

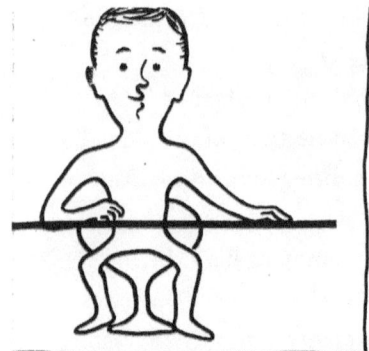

on, man bears a potential that if realized would more than satisfy the personnel demands of management;

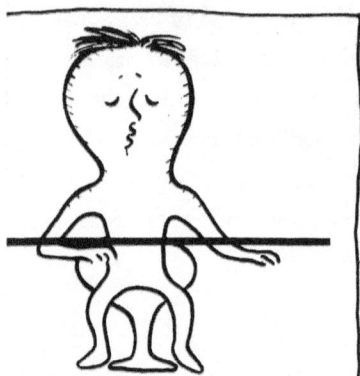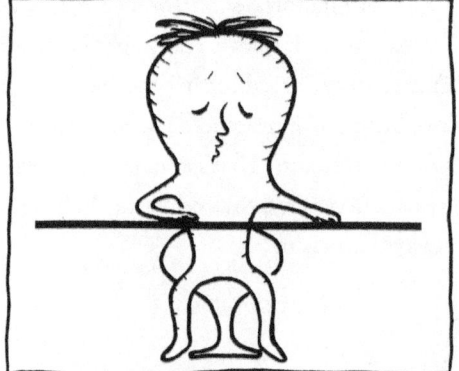

ld unbelievably escalate management's demands. From that moment on, however, man's genetic wherewithal

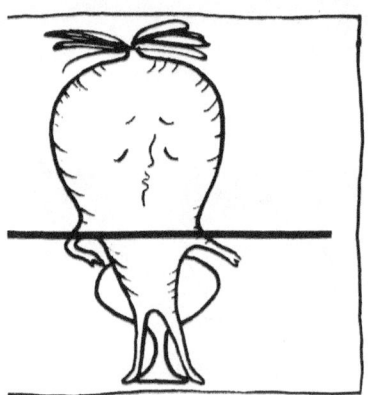

' environmental stimuli . Deprivation of environmental stimuli can turn man into a mental turnip, or worse still,

Catie Rosemurgy / *The Wondering Class*

I think the stomach means we cannot love one another properly.

I think the stomach is our one true eye.

I think the stomach is an ingredient.

I think the fingers mean we are too small inside one another.

I think the fingers mean our roots became bone and we lurched away
with a new agenda.

I think the eyelash means we can float to the ground like snow.

I think the eyelash means we must not appear burned.

Some of us have been burned, but that is not what the eyelash means.

It is unprepared for. It is the other side of the world.

The other side of the world is intricate with the lace of forests.

The other side of the world is a euphemism for disease.

I think disease means the cells have rearranged to mirror some-
     thing fast and jagged
approaching from the sky.

I think disease means full expression.

I think disease means the river truly was as golden as it seemed.

THE HOUSE BEAUTIFUL COMPETITION FOR A THREE THOUSAND DOLLAR HOUSE. IT WILL BE SEEN THAT THIS PLAN IS DESIGNED FOR A FIFTY FOOT, CORNER, TOWN LOT. THE DINING ROOM HAS BEEN RAISED TWO STEPS ABOVE THE HALL AND SITTING ROOM ; THE KITCHEN BEING ON A LEVEL WITH THE FORMER ALLOWS WHAT IS DONE FOR APPEARANCE IN THE ONE CASE, BE TURNED TO ADVANTAGE IN THE OTHER BY AFFORDING BETTER LIGHTED LAUNDRY FACILITIES IN THE BASEMENT, AS WELL AS RENDERING THE LATTER EASIER OF ACCESS FROM THE YARD OUTSIDE. MENTION MIGHT ALSO BE MADE OF THE UTILITARIAN AD-VANTAGE OF COMBINING A CENTRAL HALL FIREPLACE WITH RECESSED KITCHEN RANGE FLUES, THEREBY OBTAINING CONVENIENCE OF OPERATION AND CONTROL OF ODORS IN COOKING. WHILE AT THE SAME

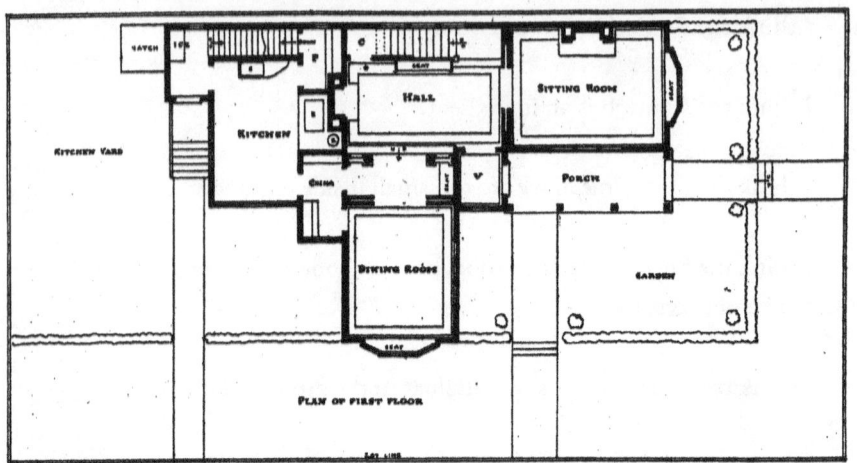

PLAN OF FIRST FLOOR

TIME AFFORDING DESIRABLE LOCATION OF FIREPLACE IN HALL THE HOUSE IS PLANNED FOR A SOUTH AND EAST EXPOSURE, THE PRINCIPAL WINDOWS OF BOTH DINING AND SITTING ROOM FACING THE GARDEN.

THE HOUSE BEAUTIFUL COMPETITION FOR A THREE THOUSAND DOLLAR HOUSE.

THE SERVANTS' QUARTERS ARE PLACED IN THE ATTIC, THE ARRANGEMENT OF STAIRCASES BEING SUCH THAT THEY MAY BE ENTIRELY CLOSED OFF FROM THE REST OF THE HOUSE IF SO DESIRED,

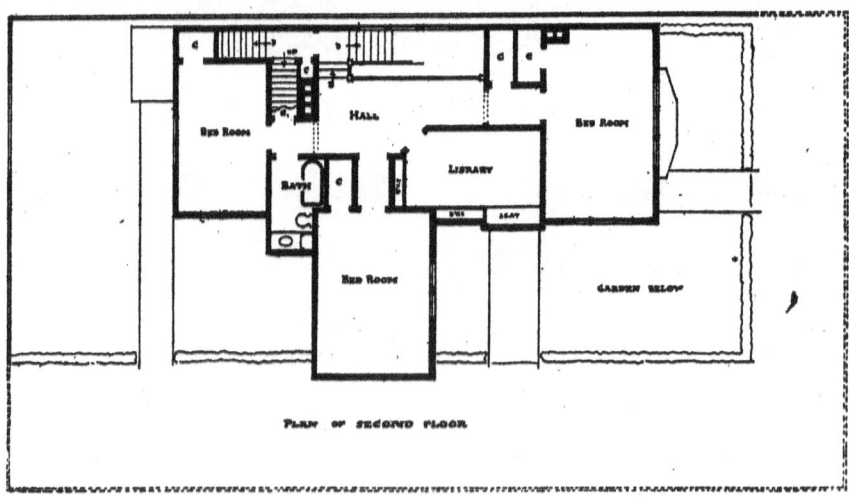

PLAN OF SECOND FLOOR

Justin Runge / *The Chart of Endings*

Here below, the pithy final acts and false epiphanies to forty unrealized stories in whose titles are formulated by the noun phrase of the X axis and the adjectival one of the Y.

	THE ARTIST	THE HOUSE YOU BUILT	THE BLOND CHILD	A FORD MODEL T	MY SORRY DREAMS
ON FIRE	No—his oil paints, with the flirtation of a fallen cigarette as he slept. •••	The scents familiar: lumber, plaster, dried and cracking bracken, all made kindling.	How the glen arched, a great back. How the blond child darted for the low lake. •••	It barreled down the infant highway, the stature of a rampaging chimney. •••	Joy had broken out across my face. "This was the house you built," the artist said. •
IN TEARS	The Seine's lapping, coupled with the foot-flattened lavender, overwhelmed him.	Could the house have buckled in response? Could the pipes have moaned, bed-ridden? ••	The buzzing arcade, the musty topcoats, pressed on her. "My mother is busy."	On that city block, the two counted every sputtering thing in earshot. Either four or five.	The sponge of his ungroomed beard saturated. He continued down the hall in a mutter.
AS AN ORPHAN	Here was an echoing, a return to the sisters' chapel hollows, when he felt first near-silence.	She drew in her margins around the walls, a scorched earth, outlasting you.	She drew in her margins schematics of the very same bed sheet escape rope.	Thomas strained his sight into the gallery forest. Yes, this is an odd place for monuments.	I hid from the nuns in a copse alee, clothes charred, linens swaying from my window.
WITHOUT LIMBS	Toppling the buckets with his chin, he went about another failed masterpiece, slathered.	No reaching out. The trees had been plucked from the ground, baring the colonnade.	"Jesus came into His dominion swaddled the same as you, Leslie." The bell.	Cranks and keys in the attic hadn't felt slots or ignitions for years, resolutely rusting.	No room was adorned. No song orchestrated. Our races were run with our tongues.
80 YEARS OLDER	She finds him, the cabernet finishing it's trickle from the wide tip of his glass, his hush.	"The stucco feels like skin," you said. We left you there, stumbling your fingers in the dimness. ••	Holes of various sizes molded into the cigar box. The ring, buried in the peat of letters.	Where had they run, in the blurry, dense winter, that could not be trailed closely.	Cinematography, needle and wax reciprocating—the last methods of my histories.
WITHOUT MEMORY	"Such an ungroomed beard." Such an ungroomed beard." This continued down the hall.	We could only approximate the portrait's dimensions from the fade of the wallpaper.	She emerged from the dense rack of discount blouses, startling the two women.	"Rend the upholstered bench, the leather canopy. Shatter the headlamps and snap the crankshaft. Yes, boys. Excise its face." And they went about it, their clubs in percussion. •••	
SUBMERSED	The Seine's lapping, coupled with the foot-flattened lavender, overwhelmed him.	As the waters, like late afternoon shadows, rise. One slate shingle surfaces.	The indigo and onyx. The gargled keen of barges above. I see the sun, obsoleting.	A dusty contrail gracefully curved to the river surface. Now to walk in the dusklight.	The portrait recovered, hung on the wall. Just in time for the rising shadow and water.
IN LOVE	For each broken tip of charcoal, the two laughed. He resharpened in slow strokes. •	The plumes of dust, the swinging of the great cobalt ball, are something operatic.	Curtains were a perfect hiding place, and in their pleats she felt drawn and anonymous. •	How the glen arched, a great back. How the blond child darted for the low lake. •••	A fallen cigarette. Near-silence. The foot-flattened. The lots of onyx. The bell.

LEGEND TO THE CHART OF ENDINGS.

This ending, although superficially sanguine, has an undercurrent of hopelessness sufficing for blood in its veins, so much so that the figurative skin of this novella assumes a starched palate of blue hues.

Any supposed animism derived from this tale is a leaden blame that sits solely on your, the reader's, shoulders, indicating your fervent wish to find qualities human in the sterile inventions that buck us.

You manifest the ensuing disaster that scripts its way in the blank pages post this declaration, in your impulse to actualize the cruel god of your manner that hopes it may exert a power unfamiliar and base.

•
••
•••

A. K. Scipioni / *Betty One: How to Make Pies*

Because pie makes two:
Layer through.
Layer. Bake. Layer.
Annie ambles. Betty wavers.
Do you need me? Layer. Pie makes
Two. Layer soft. Layer few. Annie
Layers. Betty, too. *Likeasandwich.*
Stone. Dirt. Pound. Makes
Two. Layer through. Small pan.
Set. Pie. Bake. Waver. Betty wavers.
Betty bakes. Stick
And done. Upside waif. Ready bake.
Done? And make. Till done. Till done. My
One. Betty, done? Wait. Betty weight. Annie
bates. Annie shapes. *Likeasandwich.* On
Top. Hold. And over. Betty, over. A plate
On top the other. Betty lover. Betty mother.
Dress it. And wake. Annie ambles. Betty
Shakes. Betty layers. To take. Pan,
Betty. Bake. Rambling, love. Betty.
Bake. Layer few. Makes two. Ambling.
Small till smaller. Few. Set in. Bake.
Make two. Annie ambles. Betty
Wakes. *Likeasandwich.* Plate. Pie. Top.
Annie ambles. Betty mops. Annie ambles.
Good girl. Stop. Betty top. Rambling.
Love. Amble. Dirt. Stone.
Pie. Pound. Water and sift. Water, Betty.
Water. Bake Father. Girl. Layer make.
Daughter. Betty wanders. Betty wanders.
Annie ambles. Annie saunters. Good
Good. Daughters. Likeasandwich. To

Boston, Betty? Boston? Betty sway.
I would go. I would gray. Betty say.
Say. Betty. Sift. Unsift, you say?
How else? Flour. Bake. Stone, stay. Betty
Amble. Betty. Way. Stone. Stay. Lone.
Lay. Betty. Way. Stop. Sift. Betty. Stiff.
Lifting Betty. Shift. Betty lift. Betty lift. Waver.
Wake. Waver. Annie ambles. Betty layers. Lift.
Like layer. Pebble. Girl. Waver. Makes two. Two.
Layers. *Likeasandwich*, Betty. Stay.

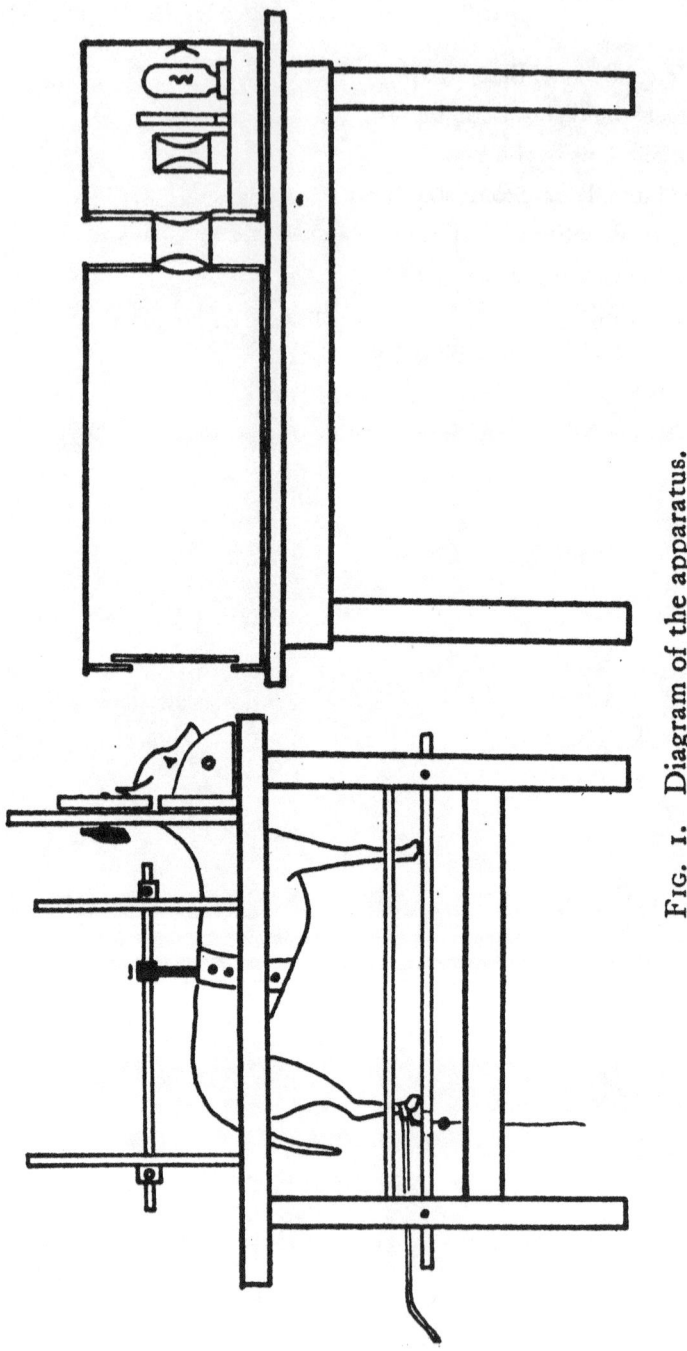

Fig. 1.   Diagram of the apparatus.

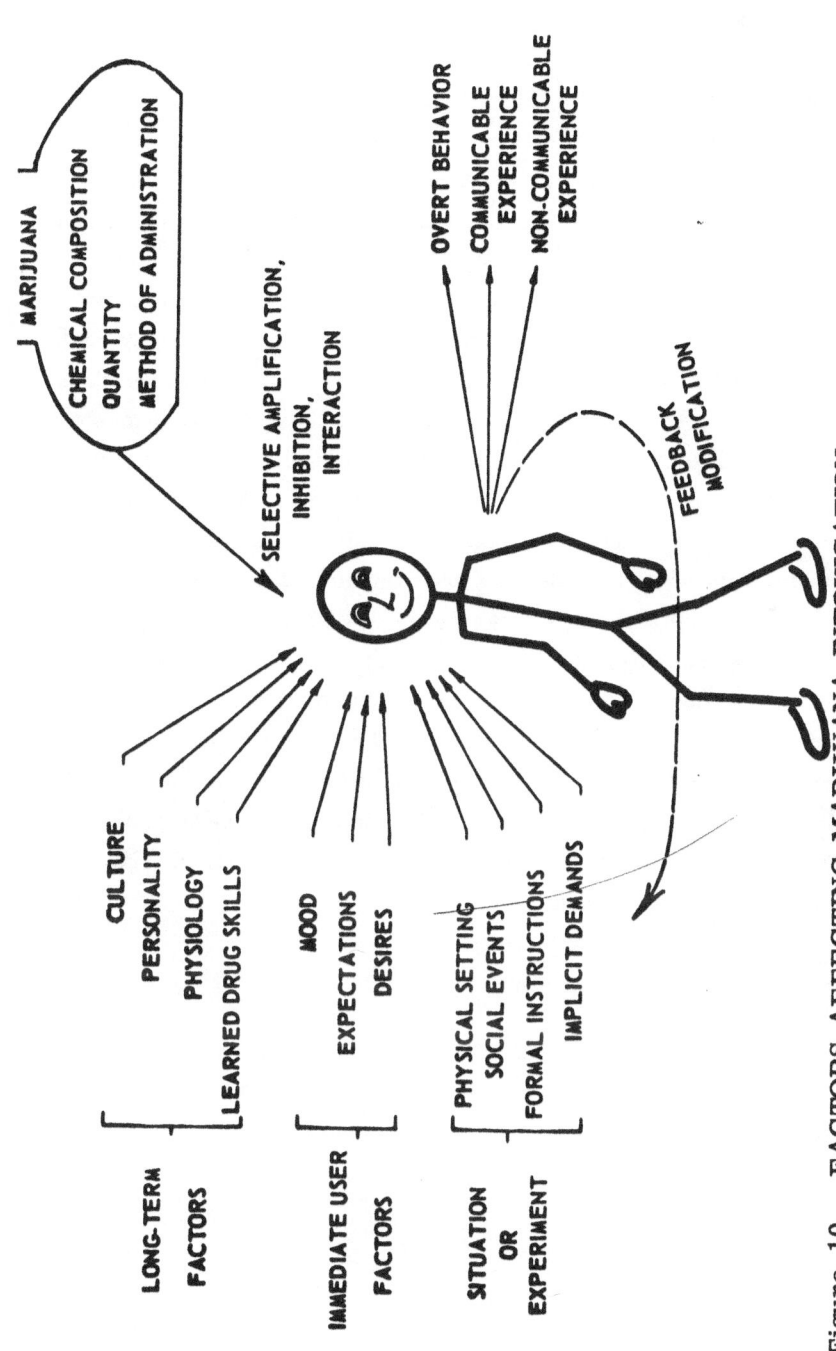

Figure 10. FACTORS AFFECTING MARIJUANA INTOXICATION

Glenn Shaheen / *Scientist*

My girlfriend and I are looking to have a child. Another lesbian couple
we know who recently got pregnant tells us of the sperm bank they went
to. They were, they assure us, given the sperm of a scientist who also is a
competitive ballroom dancer. We act giddy about how wonderful that all
is. When we get home, we tell each other that it is totally ridiculous. First,
who is a scientist and a competitive ballroom dancer? Second, even if there
is some guy who is both of those things, what is he doing selling sperm for
$50 a cup down at the clinic? When we go to the sperm bank they tell us it
is, insurance pending, $1000 for a scientist. We say we're looking for some-
thing in the $100 to $200 range. They say we can get a bricklayer, plumber,
or unemployed schoolteacher. We think we at least admire the honesty of
those people. We decide to ask a friend of ours for help. He initially seems
willing until we tell him what we need from him. Then, he gets nervous.
He is lonely. He says his parents are growing distant. He is not a scientist,
but minored in astronomy. He is not a competitive ballroom dancer, but
knows the robot better than anyone we know. When the baby is born we
lose contact with our friend. It's the kind of thing that happens eventually.
When we are in our sixties a mutual friend tells us his body was found in
his apartment. We go to the funeral. Our son is now in med school. The
mechanics of it all were crushing. We wrote a beautiful letter of sincerest
thanks and never mailed it.

Nate Slawson / *You Are Paul Newman*

I be yr horse
to whip & to
hold, not corpse,
not busted ankle
bone, & down
my throat you
can plug every
dime every
quarter, so I be
yr parking meter
& you be my
pipe cutting tool.

You Are Black Sabbath

bite my face
& I be yr dove
for all time.

You Are Saxophone

is not yr soul
a tiny jukebox,
a pain in yr heart
sprung from the
blues, & which,
when I cup my
hand to yr chest,
be like thunder-
ous rain, like
wasps in a coffee
can, & thou
nettles & dry river-
bed, thou sermon
of fire, sister, &
we hymnal of
matchsticks.

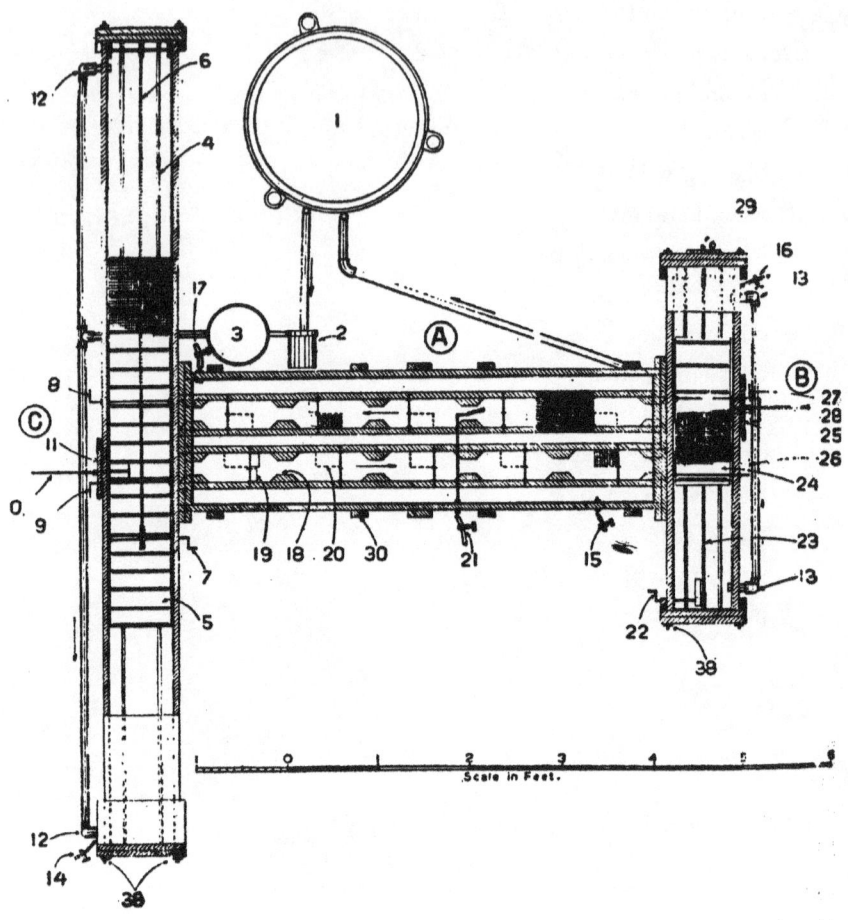

FIG. 2. TOP VIEW OF WHOLE APPARATUS

B. J. Soloy / *Acting as a Serial Correction*

Your favorite power balladeers disband,
or should. Santa Claus, James Bond, step-parent,
Superman; only stable in franchise.

In serial. The words themselves lose
form. The night bellies,
unseeming its over-worn gown.

It gets too cold to dally,
then colder.

Julie finds one white hair, then a pair
scouting around your boy bangs, which disappoints
if you'd been hoping to go instantly,

whole-hoggedly white,
no forecast. A shock.

It's not that simple, then
it is, even simpler.

Which is it?
Which is what?

That's not an answer.
That's not a question.

What are you reading?
Now I'm reading a book about rats.
Then I just up & saw a rat.
Ditto with the bird book before it.

Now a palmed cloud alights, its unlearned
limbs flapping. Birdshadow across the window,

puppeteering. Then there's bottleshell, filter-
weed, other indigenous litter. A father

with a daughter on his shoulders. The sound I make
when startled. The face I make at children.
The way I cut an onion.

It's my signature, but not my name, & it ends
on a mystery chord. The tape stops
& I'm not going to flip it again.

Waltz

This is in three
This is in four
These ballads are endearing

but unending   This traffic
a slur   Let's share
a $7.99 bottle of wine

this rumor of new weather
suddenly true
A toast:

To the species of moth that lives
entirely on cow tears
To the pigs that killed off the Dodo

To strangers as prototypes
   friends as foils
    juissance as comeuppance

I envy your orgasm(s)
Your birthday turns you
thirty And you said "right leading"

but meant light reading
I will go with you
to the tidefits

usher you in uncovered
No more city slickery
No more weeping

in the grocery store aisle light
We'll muddy the borders—
      Texhoma, Kansarado, Calexico

These are predictions
Presently, I wake up
guilty for sleeping in

You left hours ago,
your lozenges sucked small,
given up on, stuck along the sill.

Terese Svoboda / *Noble Savage*

In 1766, Jeanne Baret became the first woman to circumnavigate the world—but as a man. No one remembers her.

Her captain, Bougainville, became the first Frenchman to sail around the world. He is remembered by the bush named after him.

The difference between humans and monkeys: monkeys don't reproduce when there's no food. What they know: we're all on an island, one way or another.

Someone is pushed from a plane over an island. A woman, just as easily as a man.

A woman falls, was the first to fall.

The plane over water: looking up mirrors looking down. The plane over island: a dark cross.

After two weeks of sailing into Tahiti, Bougainville wrote: Their only god is the god of love. Paradise before The Fall.

What do monkeys dream?

Woman on a pedestal, the indigenous as Greek gods—Bougainville's journal inspired Jean-Jacque Rousseau's concept of the Noble Savage.

Guilt is what blooms after a fall. And blood.

The monkeys eat guilt, guilt that expands and fills them until they rise into the trees, until they have to catch branches to keep them from rising.

Bougainville is searching for sandalwood, that century's equivalent to oil.

As the botanist's assistant, Baret digs specimens, hauls big collection boxes on her back.

Woman are closer to nature and therefore closer to God, wrote Rousseau.

Only the Polynesians can tell the difference. They sniff Baret when her hands are full. Or are those kisses?

Beware of god reads the sign but there's always barking.

The monkeys bark.

Bougainville wrote: Women pretend not to want what they desire most. But Baret does not pretend—she is a man.

What should we do with Baret now? the sailors cry. Women on board are bad luck.

In dreams you catch yourself, you wake up.

Baret can't watch—the Polynesians are eating the mirrors Bougainville gave out.

How noble.

If we dream, are we guilty? Or is that a god's work?

A Vietnamese general interested in oil pushes a French journalist out of a plane. It is a woman, a woman's body. She is not remembered.

A fall is always political, a body stands in the way.

We stand on that island, covering ourselves.

This is not paradise, say the monkeys.

What? What? We can't hear them.

They put her off. Swim, Baret, there's your island. She reaches Marseilles.

The monkeys eat while someone falls.

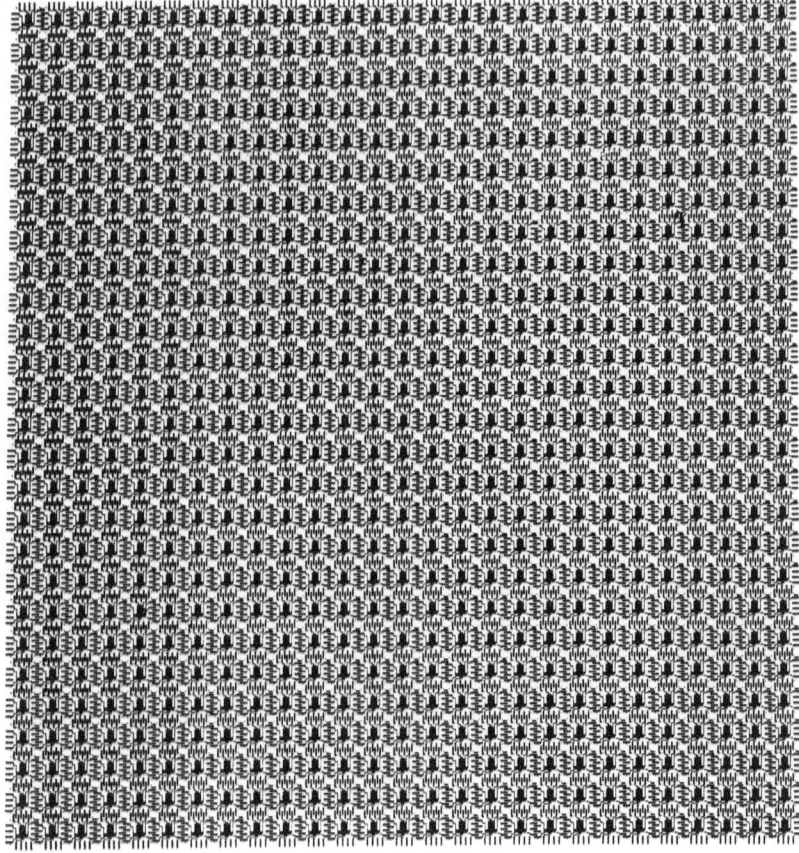

Fig. 11—Mask level containing an array of 27 × 27 of the patterns shown in Fig. 9.

No. 26: Sandy blond hair, in his twenties, with a red baseball cap. Grinned when I took out my notebook.

No 131: Very tall. Jean jacket and grey sweatshirt. Stopped to chat briefly. "I'm married, doll."

No. 79: In his sixties, wearing oxfords and a three-piece suit—no tie. Tipped a straw bowler. Frowned at me when I asked to see his hands, when I asked the color of his eyes.

No. 17: Big beer belly. Wore a button: "Lose weight now—ask me how."

No. 82: Red-faced with a big mustache. "What's this all about?"

No. 101: Hairy fingers clutching a plaid wool coat. "Jesus loves you, daughter."

No. 79 is back. Brought me a cup of coffee. Sits in the parking lot in his car.

No. 33: Scraggly beard and red hair. Laughed when I asked where he was on the night of September 23rd. "I gotta ask my wife!"

No. 64: Mid-forties. Didn't walk toward the factory, but went out to the street. Had a cocker spaniel on a leash. Let me pet her. "Isn't she soft?"

No. 145: Baseball cap that said "Toto's." Asked about my notepad. Gave me a dollar.

No. 79 is back. Nice face, balding. Brought me flowers.

No. 16: Dirty nails, plaid pants and a parka. "Get a job."

No. 65: Shaved head, one blue vein throbbing on his left temple. "Let me see your titties."

No. 79 approaches me and asks why I stand at the factory gates at the edge of the parking lot. I look into his puzzled grey eyes and I tell him that I am waiting for someone. He has brought me flowers again, daisies, and he holds them tightly in his clean, soft hands. I ask him a question and he frowns, turns away from me. Asking helps me remember, even a few fleeting seconds—moments of fading in and back out again. Was it you?

It wasn't. It wasn't No. 79, but maybe it was. I keep asking. When I ask I remember black barbed branches swaying in the wind. I remember the final rays of sun on the windows of the factory, so many windows, some blazing, some already black.

Imagine a girl, slender, with long, dark hair, two eyes, blue, wearing a short green dress and strappy shoes, a girl with hard, white teeth, crunching ice cubes in a bar. Not square four-sided cubes, but round lozenges. And she smiled at the Chipped One.

My fingers gripped the handle of a car door as I lay on the back seat. "Get out," he said.

I turned to see the factory huge in the moonlight, its black windows gaping. I remember the green fronds down by the river. The fronds brushed my arms as we trod on marshy ground.

He left bruises blooming dark and ominous across my thigh.

I, underneath, I, underwater, I came floating up, scuttling, sloshing, pulled by the underwater tug, still I came floating up into silver foam.

There was a witness, according to Captain Sergeant, someone who made a report but refused to give his name. He said only that he worked at the factory. What did he see? He saw a body in a body of water, he saw a body bobbing amid bubbles, in slick water, in the gentle but insistent surge.

Men's hands are worth noting. One had a broken finger—the other one. I remember how it stuck out at an odd angle as he held his drink. And their eyes—watch where their eyes go when they're talking to you. The Chipped One, the one who smiled at me, his eyes were made of millions of icy blue slivers. The left eye floated, unmoored, in its blue orbit, like a wobbly planet. These things I have not forgotten.

A partly submerged tire, a clear glass bottle broken at the neck, an overturned shopping cart, mired. Beneath the aqueduct, the pilings rose above me and moss edged between layers of stone. A blue-green patina of algae bloomed in the seams.

I remember rolling, turning, a gentle, lilting turning, a slow waking.

I told Captain Sergeant about crunching my ice and sipping my drink, and the numbing, swooping blankness. I told him about being carried to the car, my eyes open and then shut. I told him there were two. I told him I remember holding the glass of vodka—and then the next thing was crouching under the chain-link fence. And the river.

My shoes are in my hands.

No. 79 sits in the parking lot in his car. He tells me it is a 1965 Buick Goldstar. He invites me to sit in the passenger seat, to rest. He looks out toward the horizon. *Bless this land,* he says. His eyes are a deep, velvety grey-blue and when he talks they drift and shimmer somewhere far off and he doesn't look at me at all. He tells me he used to play the clarinet in a Salvation Army band and wore a *jacket with gold braid.* He tells me that when he was a boy his father wore *a fedora with a black grosgrain band. My dear,* he says to me, *allow me to drive you home. Were you the witness,* I ask, but he says *no.* He never saw a body in a body of water, he's never been past the chain-link fence. I have a lot more work to do, I am not done with any of them yet.

This is what's left of that night: one green dress, packaged on a shelf in the office of Captain Sergeant. One glass bottle broken at the neck. A green-foil wrapper imprinted with the word Andes. The little shiny green square was plastered to my neck, the shattered glass bottle was what I grasped in my hand. My dress is evidence now, my fish-scaled, moldering dress, reeking of chemicals, silver-green, a meadow green grassy dress, a blasted Easter basket, woven with fronds and threadbare threads. It is the dress I died in and the one in which I lived again.

Each day I stand in the parking lot with the factory behind me. I walk past blocks and blocks of empty lots and chain-link fences and warehouses to get here. I am the girl in the blasted green dress, with long, streaming hair, and dripping eyes. I still know how to smile and that is what they really want. I still know how to dream and even now my dreams are my own. I do not dream of the wavering mouths of fishes, of being buoyed up on the bumpy backs of frogs, of slimy silver eels, of the webbed feet of mallards. I do not dream of the beaks of terns plucking brackish streaks of green from my hair.

The Chipped One brought me to this lot. He and the other one carried me past the factory windows and through the chain-link fence, down to the rushing, silver river. I remember his eyes, made of a millions chips of blue light, I remember his chipped front tooth, his chipped, bitten fingers. I am the silver river girl, the dripping, drowning girl, the one who did not die.

"I like bodies," he said.

Imagine being held in water, covered with spume, spinning green and not dying. Imagine sleeping on dark silt beds, floating on currents, spinning deep and rising on black, cold waves. The witness, perhaps he knows how that could be, how I survived that night.

I saw windows, hundreds, thousands, perfect quadrangles, silver-white in the moonlight. As I ebbed and flowed in the dark waters, the factory was still, but when I awoke it had resumed its roaring, pumping discharge and the wind ruffled the silver water and the smoke and mist rose on the river.

I lay partly on the bank and partly in the water and the mist rose and rolled over me. I looked up at black branches against a silver sky as I lay there with the water still lapping at my left arm and left leg. Birds alighted in the branches and then took wing. A clear glass bottle lay in the sand by my right hand, so close that I could almost reach out and touch the broken neck of the bottle, and then I could—my fingers reached out and grasped the clear glass.

Captain Sergeant, he of the long, thin hands, hands too delicate to be those of a captain or a sergeant, he of the muddy brown eyes that never wavered—except once. He told me that the river had no name, and he raised an eyebrow and folded his long, thin hands when I told him I did not know the name of the Chipped One. And then his eyes drifted far away from me when he spoke of bloodstains and semen, and they traveled back again, to rest on me, on my face, as he told me my dress had been brined, with me in it, and that it therefore offered no secrets, only oily river water and smoke. *You're one lucky lady*, he told me.

I told Captain Sergeant it was dark and I was kneeling in the river muck, then standing, then falling again. I told him that the factory loomed behind wire fencing, that blood trickled from my knee and wrist and that the fence was broken, twisted. I told him that I was gasping and retching and being alive. He looked right at me and he didn't say anything. Then he told me that he would need to keep my dress. He said there was a witness, someone who saw but did not give his name. *That's lucky, too*, he said.

No. 79 sits in the parking lot of the factory in his Buick Goldstar, his hands folded on his stomach. He invites me to sit in the passenger seat. He tells me that he's retired now, but that he parked in this lot every day for 22 years. He turns his kindly grey eyes to me, but then he looks out again and his eyes change, they get clear and chilly, and I wonder what he has seen, what he knows. I want to remind him of the swirling eddies of the river and all it contains, but I don't because then his eyes come back, they get cloudy with concern and his brows are like black hillocks looming over the grey.

I keep asking my questions and taking my notes and so far I have ruled out Nos. 26, 48, 55, 63, 76, 91, 92, 103, 106, and 112. Asking keeps me windy inside, like the *golden prairie* that No. 79 tells me about, like the soft, green pastures rolling out to the blue horizon, like *papa's white shirts on the clothesline*, like the way his heart soared *to see my mama standing there*.

The Chipped One, his hands were like wild birds fluttering in all the crevices of my being. I tell that to No. 79 but he shows no sign of recognition. If he stumbled upon that scene, maybe he would never tell. But I keep asking. As long as I keep asking, then I do not dream of huge stone pilings made of schist soaring above me. I do not dream of bloody chain-links and wrecked, spindly trees; I do not dream of smelting sparks and embers and bonfires.

Each day now I sit with No. 79 in the Buick. He tells me his name is Henry William Gastemeyer, but I don't call him that. I don't call him anything. I'm sound as a clock, he says, and thumps the steering wheel. He tells me that he remembers every word his mother ever said to him. I tell him that I need a witness, that I need someone who can remember what he saw. I tell him that I am collecting slivers and shards and strands.

I remember sounds, ones I'd been hearing all along—birds, far-off traffic, the laplaplap of the river.

What I know is that in the deeper place of the river, there are soft white fronds, long grey eels, catfish with whiskers floating on the currents, clumps of moss and tangled river weeds. Over all this, a sweet gray smoke holds sway, a rising chemical mist hovers over the water and burns the lungs.

I've stopped asking No. 79 any more questions because asking makes him quiet and I want to keep him talking, I want to rest in the vast, windy grey of his eyes, I want to hear about how the plow churned up *newly turned earth*, how the *swallows swooped out of the trees* and how his heart soared *to see my mama standing there*. He brought her *fistfuls of Michaelmas daisies and Queen Anne's Lace*, and she put them into the pockets of her calico apron, stalks and stems and dirt still clinging to the roots. *She shooed me away*, he says. But he stayed and she turned back to him and drew him to her. "Land's sake," she said and drew him closer.

"Was it you?" I ask him, and he nods. But when I ask him what he saw, he just shakes his head. I tell him, Imagine the body of a girl bumping along in the undertow. She is bathed in silt, her hair streaked with algae, and she breathes in vapors and mists. She rises radiant from a slurry of isotopes and polymers, she rises toward the oxygen, she staggers up into silt and loam, her hair rank and steaming, rivulets of flotsam coursing from her dress, oozing from every orifice.

I stand at the entrance to the parking lot, by the factory, in a different dress, my hair lank and unwashed. I have been steeped in deep waters, nudged by the gentle mouths of eels, grazed by the underbellies of frogs, mired in the soft, sodden muck of rotten leaves. The silver slurry of no-name river left its imprint on me: my breath comes a little harder now, my eyes are the cool, watery eyes of a not-drowned girl, my fingers tremble now, sometimes I can't feel my feet at all, my spine rattles, my skin is translucent.

No. 79 walks me partway to the river. We get almost all the way there. He is gallant and gentlemanly, offers me his arm. As we walk, I tell him that I need a witness. He doesn't say anything, but he turns to me, up close, and his eyes are narrow, his brows hunkered down over them. I urge him on, thinking that if we get there, he'll give himself away, he'll tell everything he knows. I tell myself to breathe as deeply as if these were my last breaths. No. 79 looks everywhere but at me; he stares at the pewter sky smoldering before us. And there is the river, just as it was. He turns back.

No. 79 has asked to see my notes, and I turn over the 86 pristine pages. He scans them before handing them back. I tell him that these are my notes of that night, the night for which there is no evidence, nothing that is not steeped in chemical brine. I tell him that these are the minutes of that night, from which minutes and hours and more are missing, and I wait. He stares straight ahead.

No. 79 parks the car amid the fronds, by the fence, and I get out. He stays behind the wheel, and when I look back the car seems to hover there amid the fronds, silver in the gloaming. He opens the door and gets out, he stands with the door open and calls to me. "You mustn't cross," he tells me, and points to the No Admittance sign by the fence. I tell him that I need to get to the river. "It's not much of a river, miss," he says.

I remember the glittery mosaic of the Chipped One's eyes, even in darkness. The factory was at my back and I was on my knees in sand. Something came out of my mouth—a throaty slur before swooping back into darkness. Then I remember morning and the sun heating up the high grass. I remember birdsong.

I am not afraid. I know the way back in through the twisted links of the fence. I know the way the trees lean out over the river. I know the river's shallows and its depths, I know where it forks, I know where its bottom rises up, I know where a slender body can float and shimmer in those waters, I know how to stop breathing and then breathe again.

I don't know how I slept in those waters, how I swam, or scuttled, or breathed with water breath, how I made my way. Perhaps I parted the reeds, navigated the eddies and sloughs, and rode the quickening currents all night long. I took what the river gave me, I breathed in flakes of soot and ash, I inhaled one bright bubble at a time, and I lived.

Captain Sergeant held some papers in his thin, white hands and read aloud and shook his head. "You're one lucky lady," he told me.

I lead No. 79 past plastic bags and discarded syringes, under the blue-green pilings. He scans the horizon, as he always does. Then he looks down when he realizes he has splashed into the water. He backs away as the water engulfs his shoes. He offers me his arm. "I'd like to walk you home," he says.

"I take note of your tears," he says. He steps away from the water and stumbles on the stubby, stony bank. But then he turns and comes back toward me. He stares at me, his eyes dark pinholes. I don't move. Do you remember a girl like me, I ask him, only silver-green and waterlogged and streaked with dirt and tears? Do you remember a girl spinning and drowning and rising again? He doesn't answer. I keep one foot on the bank and one in the water. He turns, tips his hat, and moves back toward shore. He won't try to stop me.

The trees lean over the water, spreading their splintered branches, the birds sing their uneven song, the waters slap against the schist, leaving a scummy rime, a sparrow stalks the shore, spreading its metallic wings, a cold wind crests on the rugged, silver waves. All things that settle here, in these waters, on these banks—prepare to bear witness to a shivering, riven, surfacing girl.

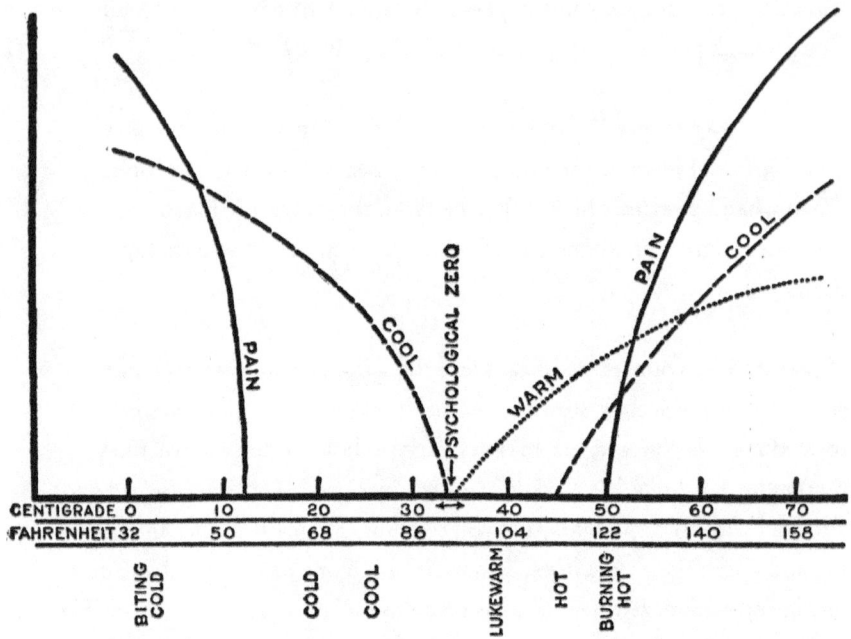

FIG. 68. DIAGRAM TO SHOW THE RELATIONSHIP BETWEEN THE TEMPERA-
TURE OF THE SKIN AND INTROSPECTIVE EXPERIENCE

22. the   rupture   passed
            skin or sand | a
    soft trickling   against
                      smooth glass
          pink,   green,   darken

23.   Acute at   tongue
          burned   skin,   a
       mass of   smoke   rolled
          over
                      nerves
          flashes of ecstatic light

24. midst the   layers, lipid
        shaking at, the   sterile
    needle,   skin   opening
        words   pouring in
        divine white   blood-cells

25. pale   skin at   eye
                level   closer, below
        deform   a   jagged edge
                of cells   blooming

26. puncture   seal of
        soft red   a
    leg muscle   swell
            skin   rises
    curving   to   gold
            cloud-shape

27. black flame from sky
            to skin ark is
        engraved arm
            scars a border   the
    ink stains   raised

28. abscess   a flower growth
          system's   strange glow
    flux of   birdsong
          beneath the skin

                              29. cords   flutter heavy   at
                          breath   tips broken, move
                                  in corners,   halting
                      body
                          grey skin   sinks, gently

30. foam at   mouth
        eye   whites
    coldskin   trembles
              to push   out
a ghost
          or legion

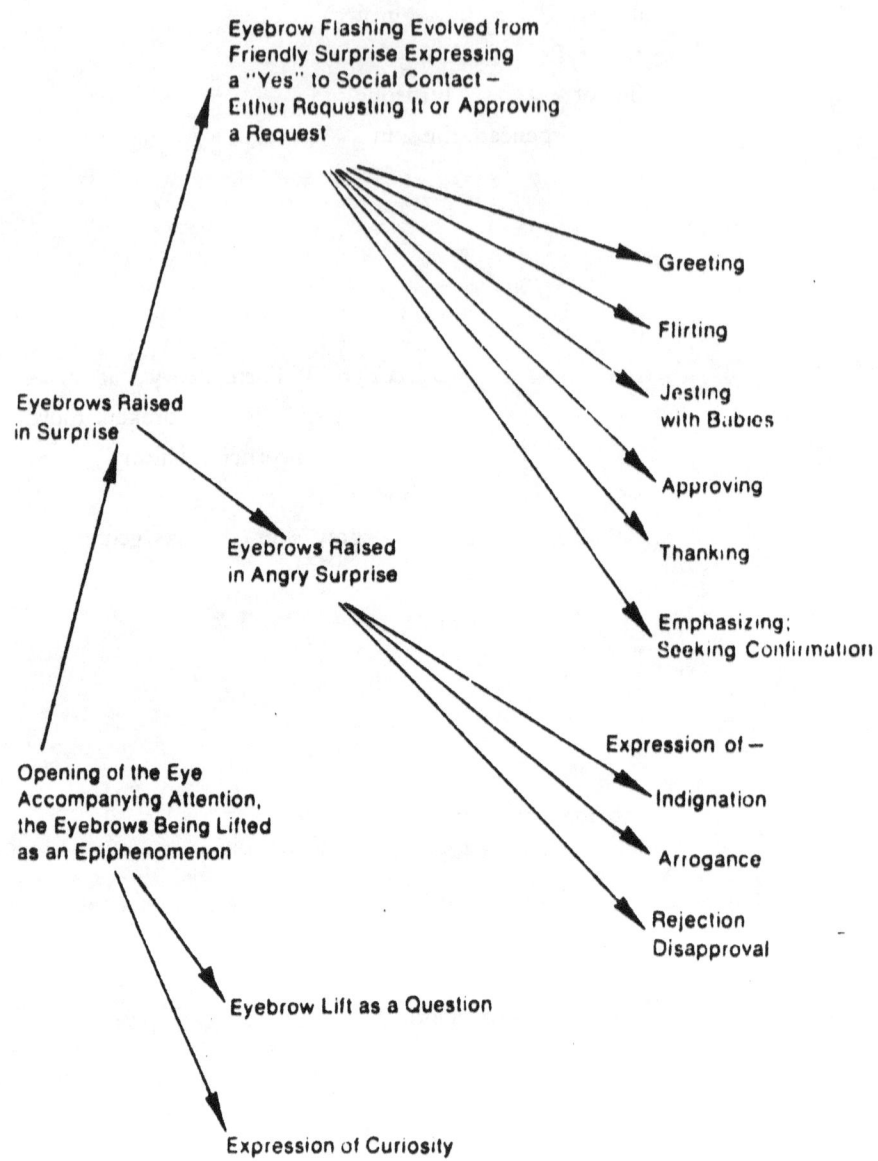

Eyebrow Flashing Evolved from
Friendly Surprise Expressing
a "Yes" to Social Contact –
Either Requesting It or Approving
a Request

Greeting

Flirting

Jesting
with Babies

Approving

Thanking

Emphasizing:
Seeking Confirmation

Eyebrows Raised
in Surprise

Eyebrows Raised
in Angry Surprise

Expression of –

Indignation

Arrogance

Rejection
Disapproval

Opening of the Eye
Accompanying Attention,
the Eyebrows Being Lifted
as an Epiphenomenon

Eyebrow Lift as a Question

Expression of Curiosity

Michael Walsh / *Grounding*

Ticking louder
against the electric fence,

weak in the crossed mess of stems,
weeds break under your stick.

An underground signal
beats in their roots.

Brush a leaf, a wire by accident
and you turn the wrong dial.

The sudden, terrible sun
pounds the air white,

the ground black as static.
For hours after

your fingertips babble, their prints
strange as radio waves.

Landscape with Forgotten Machines

Searching the creeping charlie and wild grape
you can't tell fallen branch from axle,

barbed wire from the vine that burns
like a fuse through the tangle.

Two boxelders have twisted their trunks
through a plow's rusted frame, landlocked

the blades. On a hay rack's gray slats
a field of thick, dusty mold blooms.

Somewhere inside these thorns and burrs:
car batteries black and juicy with acid,

deflated innertubes that stick like leeches
to the dirt. And underneath the plants and junk,

rust welds together the lost washer rings.
Bolts hibernate like seeds. Screws burrow.

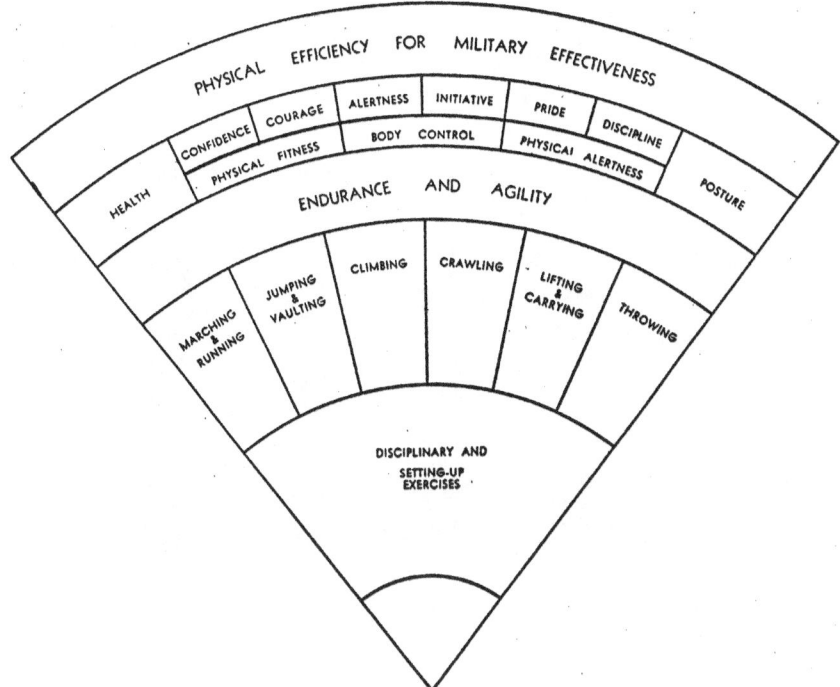

Figure 1. Chart.

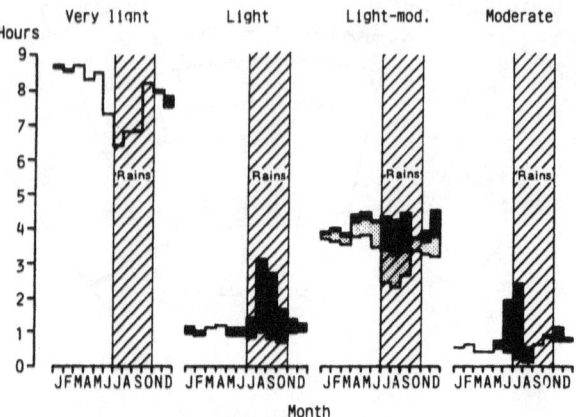

Fig. 1. *Seasonal variation in time spent at various categories of work in rural Gambian women.* Shaded area represents time spent on agricultural work, stippled area represents time spent walking to and from the fields.

Kellie Wells / The End of the World, The Wend of the Lord

(As recorded by loyal amanuensis Lord W. Drol, escort)

When the world finally ended one Thursday afternoon, brown clouds tumbling
    from the sky like potatoes shaken from a sack, I watched as the polar
        bear's paw, the very shape and size of that dooming cavity that
            opened up in the ice cap and forecast the coming of a liquid
world, struggled for purchase on a tiny ice floe, no bigger than two trout
stitched together, and then relaxed, dear bear, vanishing forever beneath the
water, sinking to the blind depths to join the rest, glub-glub, sea floor littered
with bags of bones, flattening bearskins spread about as in an alpine
ski lodge from that endless era when earthlings thought bears
were only for killing, for warming their feet. Soon the
empty bears would float to the ocean's surface
                then rise into the air like fur tippets snagged on a stiff
             gale and disappear in that torrent of final clouds, everything
         on the hazard, whoosh! They have nothing to answer for, having
    acquitted themselves honorably during their tenure on the tundra. Even
the bearded seals do not dispute this.

    The sun, reduced to a squint, cast little light across this, the dying day,
    and I watched as honeybees wafted toward a dimly greening world and
    never returned, apiaries once dutifully abuzz now vacant as a cloudless sky,
    colonies sacked by mites, pesticide, the tedium of a world gone poisonous,
    so many ways to die these days who can say, almonds cucumbers kiwis only
    an inkling inside a spinster bloom, angiosperms withering in maidenhood,
    randy daisies yearning for the sticky feet of bees (no virtue in chastity for
    a flower), and suddenly it is a world without buttercups, a world without
    apples, a world without honey! (It is a world without love, without sleep,
    without bears.)

        I watched as the sizzling green glow of a radioactive planet could find no
        one to keep awake.

Woe, woe, woe, I heard the sky sing, despair betiding the ravaged world when what we stunned stragglers grudgingly longed for, instinct getting the better of us (as instinct always does), keeping us gasping and tottering forward against our better judgment, was a yanking on the reins that could halt destruction: woe, woe, woe. There is no salvation in a Word any longer. There is no Word any longer.

I watched as the earth skinned itself like an orange. I watched as maps became irrelevant.

The sky reddened and began to drip, a pomegranate, a bloodshot eye, a bedsore on the world's backside, God's necrotic heart, and I watched as the animal rains began, deluge of creatures pummeling the earth, first small ones, just enough animal to fill a teacup or two, tree frogs and parakeets and skinks and voles and box turtles and marmots falling from falling clouds in a dark and heavy stream, then whooping cranes and lava mice and wombats and ibex and sunbears and Kansas bog lemmings and sturgeon and pumas and mysterious starlings and donkeys and emus and paradise parrots and meerkats and sea mink and cobras and tapirs and broad-faced potoroo and finally the elephant, finally the whale, finally the dinosaur, caked in ice, all manner of mammal, amphibian, reptile, and bird falling from above, a fearsome hailstorm of animal life leaving smoldering divots in the bald earth they once roamed—bewhiskered, beclawed, betailed, nocturnal, omnivorous, marsupial, extinct—meteors landing where once there were houses and heliports and gardens, natatoriums and foundries and racetracks, strip mines and penitentiaries and abattoirs, killing fields and theme parks, where once civilization happily blighted the landscape, tolde-rolloll! blinkblink!

I watched as acid fell from the sky, consigning we scatterlings to the flames, and the last sanctifying dribbles of Holy Water scalded the skin of believers and mugwumps alike.

As it turned out, this was the appointed day of God's rapture, and God rose up to meet Himself, fresh from the grave, clods of dirt, scraggly roots, beetles, the dust of long vanquished beliefs clinging to His stubbled chin, lending him an archaeological air. God confessed to the tribunal of Himself His sins—*Dear beneficent God God-God*, said God to God and. God. *sun and moon and starry sky of my ailing heart, please forgive God His many trespasses,infinite in number*, and Gods replied, with a condemning snort and a withering glare, *Yahweh or the highway, Mr. Bub!*—which confession took an eternity and eventually roused all sleeping dogs, who had slumbered through the animal squall (legs atwitch as they charged zigzagging rabbits that these days exist only in the dreams of very old dogs) but who now sniffed the ankles of the ascendant, bark! So God, that dawdler, nearly missed the Apocalypse, the Four Horsemen having long ago left the paddock, nags antsy as evolution.

    Drag a demon! God exclaimed, *no, that's not it. O mad danger! Mad dog near! no, Goddamn ear damn god ear?* no, no, something arm a-something something, *Arm a dog den!* Ack, wrong again, odsbodikins! And at this there was much howling. God stroked His prominent chin (about which He couldn't help but be a little vain, dimpled chin of a leading man, lothario, chin of a rogue, such a fetching profile, chiseled jaw of a movie star and He knew it, picked it out Himself on that day He soldered together the carcass He would inhabit for this His coming-out), and looked to the starving sky for a sign, searching the blue for the shibboleth that would reveal his Godly dialect, for the ear of wheat from which that riffraff chaff could finally be separated, high-toned imposters, counterfeit gadabouts cats cads goads cods codes cots coats goats g-g-g-gods, pleh! (Where had His language gone? Had it forsaken Him for greener gods to come? Punish polish *perish* the thought!), pretenders to the throne cast out once and for all, granting Him the great gold self-winding chronometer of His retirement, a ringside seat at the End Times tickticktickticktick, at hand at last. *Goddamn era!* spat God, shaking his fists—big as two moons and twice as dazzling—at the empyrean whence He fell once upon a prophecy, and that's when Time slammed on the brakes and we were all thrown into the breach, clocks and watches and sundials everywhere shattering, the sky filling with hands and faces, springs and gnomons and fobs, clickwheels spinning in the seasick light, sproing!

There is always a moment before the world ends when it might not have, an instant just before the mushrooming of annihilation when the end might have proven to be a dud, pffft.

2. A CAPO YELPS, A SPACE PLOY

God's abduction by extraterrestrials the previous Tuesday was not without its comforts. For a day suffering paused. (Bodies scheduled for reclamation persisted, obstinately thought some, they piled up, swooning cows stalled on the gangplank, waiting for the hammer blow to the head, waiting to swing from the hoof, waiting to be bled, lowing, lowing; mourners circled deathbeds aimlessly, handkerchiefs and black crepe and widows' weeds at the ready.) The aliens' melted bodies, skin green as a looper worm, pooling like candle wax, hovered over Him as they sliced Him down the middle with a wand of hot light, slit His puparium stem to stern (and though God was no longer larval, this halving incision insured He was forever suspended, 'twixt naught and nothing, never to reach imago, poor stunted caterpillar, alas o alas!). They cracked God open, bloodless as an apple He turned out to be, and there, where they'd hoped to find the beating heart of divinity, they found instead a note that said *You. Are. Here.* Some cardiological scalawag in some other pocket of the universe had beaten them to it, nuts! The aliens, so advanced, everyone in the universe said so, always prepared to make the best of a bad outcome, to learn from their miserable failures (that's why they could zip from one end of the cosmos to the other in the bat of an eye, vroom, teleporting from lily pad to lily pad, a happy accident that had been; well, eventually happy, a *quantum* miscalculation at first, boy-howdy, kidneys where ears should have been, ears lost to eternity, somewhere an armada of noses sneezing in the ether, floating through time; nevertheless, the irksome inconvenience of noselessness notwithstanding, the aliens, like God, knew a thing or two about intergalactic aerodynamics if they did say so themselves), noted the effeminate flourish in the *way* the *Y* and the *A* and the *H* curled round themselves, gilding their own spires (*Yah!* said the aliens, *Hay!* said the aliens, *Hey is for horses!* said God, preparing to be pithed), vines encircling a beanstalk, ensorcelling the aliens, who rubbed weak jaws with spindly green fingers, hmmmm.

Then they placed a transistor in one of God's molars so He could be easily tracked, those mysterious movements mapped (no one ever believed him, poor ragtag, irrational God, off his meds for millennia, paranoid as a snowshoe rabbit trapped white and ready in a green winter). This was, it must be said, a coup d'etat for the aliens, who, like those backwoods, gullible Earthlings, those country dumplings, greenhorns of the universe, had been looking for God since they first heard tell of him, light years and light years and light years ago, after missionaries, those gospel hucksters, newly arrived to their incinerated planet, offered their famished masses rice in exchange for belief, an a priori admission of guilt, and attendance at the occasional potluck (it had seemed such a bargain!). This was at a time when the aliens' skin still fit though not snugly, was beginning to sag, their not-yet-crumbling bones still determining the dashing drape of their flesh, which was soon to droop unbecomingly. They were hungry and therefore vulnerable to suggestion (many a convert has adapted her convictions after watching her belly round in emptiness). The callow aliens, who had not yet known devastation, unschooled in plague and war—no rival tribe nor microbe yet to develop genocidal designs on their fledgling race, no nearby god to smite or drown them, only a relentless sun with a chip on its shoulder, burning the candle at both ends—could not know that satiety is necessarily fleeting and that there isn't enough grain in the universe to keep them from turning to tallow: it is the fate of flesh everywhere. A sigh escaped God's yellowing liver.

God gathered his flesh around his remains, hiked it up to his waist like infinite bloomers, the billowing shape and weight of the universe— though some parts, so finely examined, had to be left behind: his kid-

neys, his thumbs, three ribs, and his spleen, and the aliens sold these
relics, which they promised would reverse any ailment, antidote any
grief, to the lame and hobbled slack-skinned natives puddled on the
steps of the Great Laboratory—and he sutured the shreds of himself
back together so that he could walk without tripping, so that he could
be there when each planet gave up the ghost (guilt-ridden He for
having missed so many recitals and little league games, absentee god,
deadbeat deity He), and then he lost his balance (owing no doubt to a
bout of labyrinthitis, not uncommon in a supreme being of his vintage,
the interior of God's wobbling head an unthinkable maze with no
likely egress for those big thoughts he routinely thunk), lost at long last
his longstanding battle with gravity (having packed on a few pounds
over the years), and fell straight to Earth, land ho!, where, mistaken for
irradiated space junk, he was promptly interred.

I watched as water crept up the sky and the sky lapped at the sun
and the sun stopped beating and the stars winked then went blind,
their antediluvian extinction finally reaching us at last, too late for a
proper mourning.

3. APACE, LO SPY! PLACE YAP SO:

And who am I, you may ask, Lord W. Drol, to have
watched life on Earth end and so unbountifully? I am only the
world's psychopomp, the gondolier escorting its tattered, baggy soul
across the choppy waters (chop-chop!) that lead after all to the Afterworld.
And if You are reading this, dear Deity, it stands to reason You are
God Reconstituted, risen from the ash heap, reassembled
from scraps, and though I am *long* dead, dead
as a herring, dead as the day before yesterday, beyond
yearning and desire, beyond hunger, beyond terror, beyond the
wearing of sneakers, I say to you that I hope, I *pray*, this time you will
be able to act, oh Merciful Redeemer, on that fat knowledge you hoard. Arf!

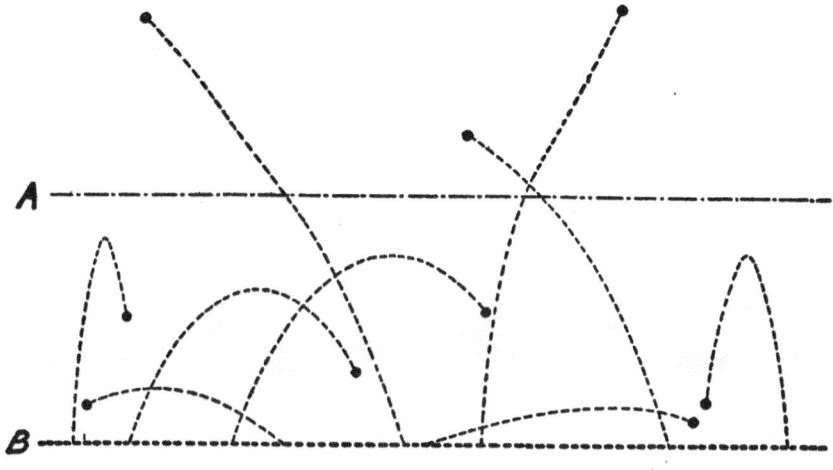

Fig. 9

VAPOR MOLECULES AT THE SURFACE OF A LIQUID

As explained in the text, the vapor which rises from the surface of any liquid consists in molecules which are shot through the film of surface attraction. Slow-moving molecules may penetrate the liquid surface but be returned to it once more by the forces of attraction. Fast-moving molecules, however, may escape permanently. The paths described by molecules of both sorts are illustrated above. *A* is the limit at which the attraction ceases to be effective for a molecule moving sufficiently fast to reach this line. *B* is the liquid surface.

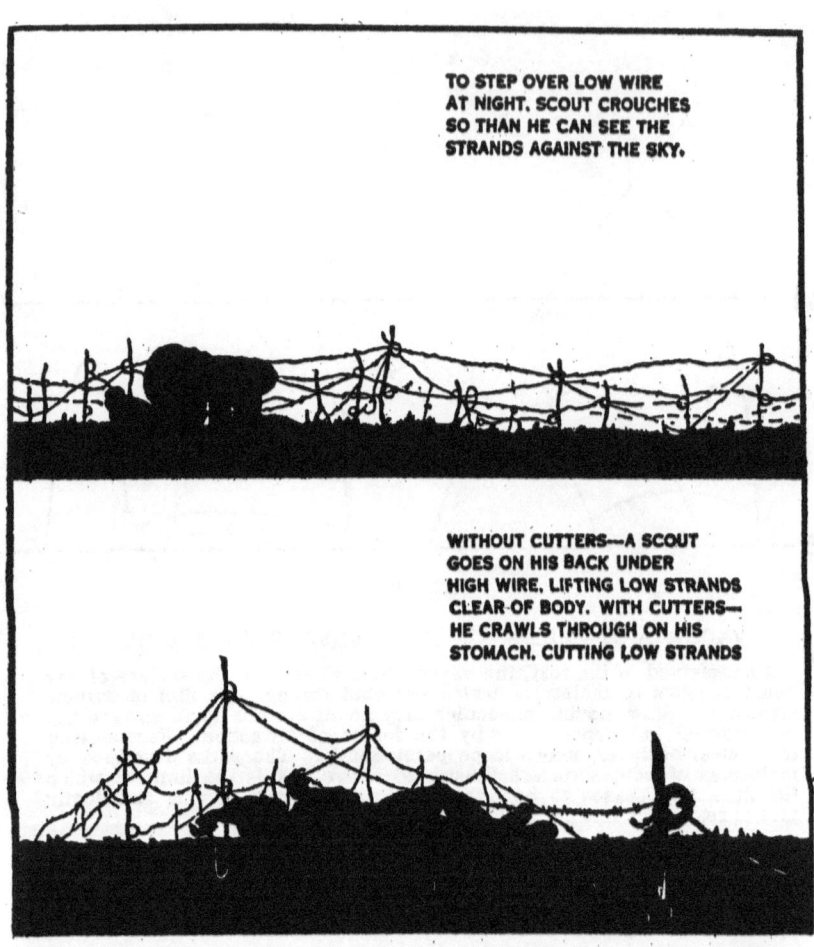

Figure 52.—Methods of Crossing Wire Silently at Night.

Cori A. Winrock / [Bias 2]

I   *You*

I.
I blow through the house—a night
(*what anatomy does*) gown of

alveoli, my lung
sacks full of voice-less

you you; laces of *this* and
ribs enclose—liſþ liſþ

I am sss
I am s

my heart is.

II.
Each morning I awake: my grief is up
already, an early

riser. My ſteps slush through.

I   you

(arctics and over-
coats) metered up a hill,
breath pressed inside

out. *My heart is.*
Is is.

My heart in the language
of the left half. *Patience, adieu.*

III.
I jot down
I burn into, line the left
cuff of my fall

dress coat. Warm paper
sewn into the hem of my sleeve:
and this and this and this and

IV.
My love,
I was—

inaccessible, we turn
from each other—a clot
shivering loose.

Joshua Jennings Wood / *Columbus's Wet Dream*

I wear the finest fabrics crafted in China, Indonesia.

I try to eat right.

I wipe beads of steam from my mirror in the morning.

I ride something to work—something mechanical.

I plan on throwing it away.

I need to look at my schedule.

I know what you're going to say.

I had it removed.

I think I want some more.

I couldn't remember if I tried.

I don't think I have time.

I felt like something new.

I might sign myself up for one of those groups, at least get on a list.

I can't say what this means to me.

I have to find a little more me time.

I hate this show.

I could lose myself in here.

I fail to see how it affects me.

I guess I don't know my limits.

I just can't finish this.

Fig. 10—Test pattern for XYMASK illustrating
sloped line capability of the pattern generator.

Bill Yarrow / *She Who Misunderstood Love*

Once in a fit of pique, she poured
vinegar on the anniversary roses
which withered in his seeing. In
retribution, he became incontinent.
That made her, she who misunder-
stood love, love him more, and him,
he who misunderstood marriage,
respect her less. Is there a recipe for
lasting happiness? Look, perhaps, to
applesauce. The apples of attraction.
The sugar of indulgence. The water of
conduction. Everything improves over
time. Everything in the world. Except
the consolidated body. Except the
orphan garden. Except ripe fruit.

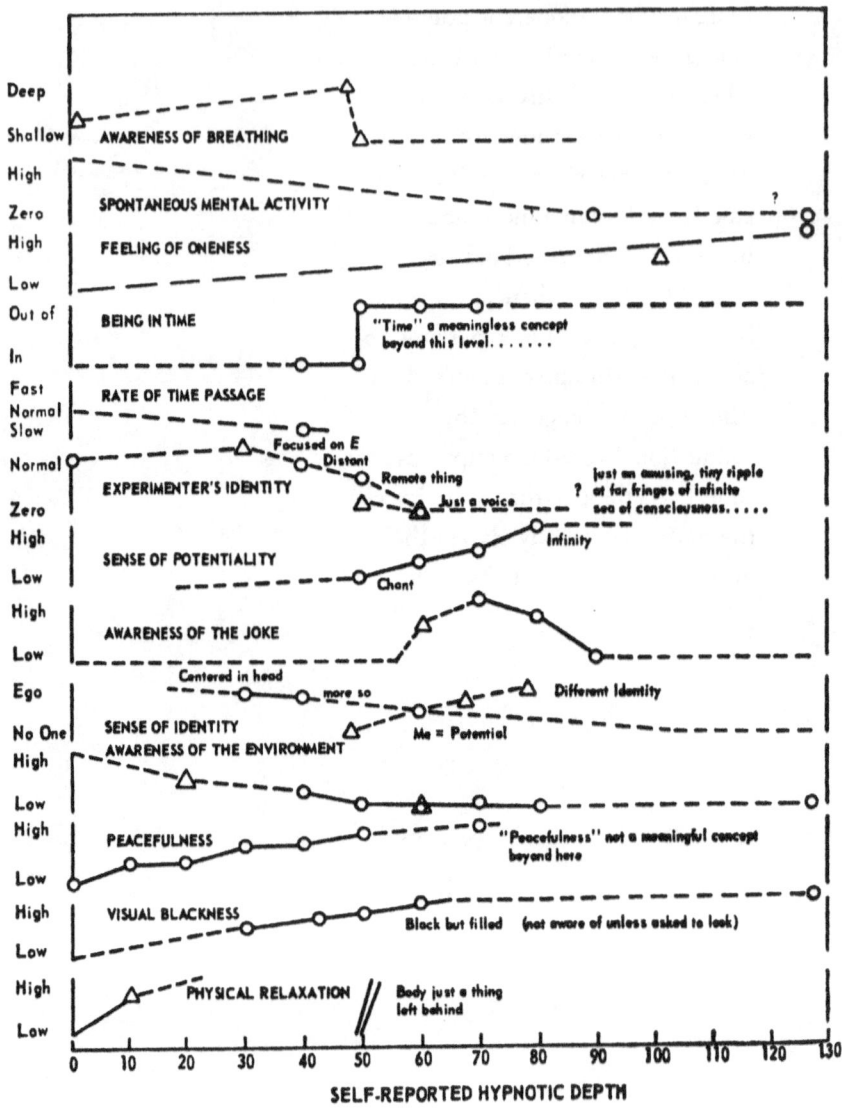

The relationship of the intensity of various experiences to self-reported hypnotic depth.

An Index to the Schematics in this Anthology

68   Stanford C. Ericksen, "Variability of Attack in Massed and
     Distributed Practice," *Journal of Experimental Psychology*, 31.4,
     October 1942.

7   "A Housekeeper's House Plan," *The House Beautiful*, 5.3, Febru-
     ary, 1899.

134   Andreas Keil, Thomas Gruber, Matthias M. Müller, Stephan
      Moratti, Margarita Stolarova, Margaret M. Bradley, and
      Peter J. Lang, "Early Modulation of Visual Perception by
      Emotional Arousal: Evidence from Steady-State Visual
      Evoked Brain Potentials," *Cognitive, Affective, and Behavioral
      Neuroscience*, 3.3, September, 2003.

18   Diana Clifford Kimber, Carolyn E. Gray, and Caroline E. Stack-
     pole, *Textbook of Anatomy and Physiology*, MacMillan, 1893.

204   M. Lawrence and R. G. Whitehead, "Physical Activity and Total
      Energy Expenditure of Child-Bearing Gambian Village
      Women," *European Journal of Clinincal Nutrition*, 41.2, Febru-
      ary, 1988.

142   J. C. R. Licklider and M. E. Bunch, "Effects of Enforced Wake-
      fulness Upon the Growth and the Maze-Learning Perfor-
      mance of White Rats, *The Journal of Comparative Psychology*,
      39.6, December, 1946.

42   Paul Mayen, "A Reminder of What We Know," *Office Design*,
     November, 1965.

166   Nicholas J. Polites, "Shaping the Human Psyche," *Office Design*,
      July, 1966.

168   "Prize Competition," *The House Beautiful*, 5.1, December, 1898.

120   Dorian Rose, "Comparison of Fetal Development in Normal and Hyperthyroid Rats," *The Journal of Comparative Psychology*, 40.2, April, 1947.

100, 160,   W. Samaroo, J. Raamot, P. Parry, and G. Robertson, "The
186, 216   Electron Beam Pattern Generator," *The Bell System Technical Journal*, 49.9, November, 1970.

128, 178   Robert O. Scow, "The Retarding Effect of Allyl Thiourea and of Partial Thyroidectomy at Birth Upon Learning in the Rat," *The Journal of Comparative Psychology*, 39.6, December, 1946.

141, 148   John H. Stokes, Herman Beerman, and Norman R. Ingraham, Jr., *Modern Clinical Syphilology*, W. B. Saunders Co., 1944.

154, 173,   Charles T. Tart, "On the Nature of Altered States of Conscious-
218   ness with Special Reference to Parapsychological Phenomena," *Research in Parapsychology*, 1973.

12   Charles T. Tart, "Space, Time, and Mind," *Research in Parapsychology*, 1977.

2, 8, 196   Howard C. Warren and Leonard Carmichael, *Elements of Human Psychology*, Houghton Mifflin, 1930.

172   Kempton G. Wing and Karl U. Smith, "The Role of the Optic Cortex in the Dog in the Determination of the Functional Properties of Conditioned Reactions to Light," *Journal of Experimental Psychology*, 31.6, December, 1942.

1   John E. Winter, "An Inexpensive Noiseless Memory Apparatus," *Journal of Experimental Psychology*, 30.4, April, 1942.

17 Yun Xu, Dorab E. Bhagwagar, Paul C. Painter, and Michael
      Coleman, "Binary Polymer Blends Involving Multiple
      Specific Interaction Sites Poly (vinyl methyl ether) Blends
      with an Ethyl Metachrylate-Co4-Vinyl Phemol Copolymer,"
      Macro-Molecular Symposia 84, 1994.

53 Safa R. Zaki and Robert M. Nosofsky, "A Single-System Inter-
      pretation of Dissociations Between Recognition and Catego-
      rization in a Task Involving Object-Like Stimuli," *Cognitive,
      Affective, and Behavioral Neuroscience*, 1, 2001.

—

Other *DIAGRAM*
Productions Include:

—

(Some From) DIAGRAM
DIAGRAM.2
DIAGRAM III
10 of DIAGRAMs, a 10th anniversary deck.

—

Except for the 10th anniversary deck,
which is only available in a limited edition
directly from NMP, all of these are available
from New Michigan Press or in bookstores.